What people are saying about

Frigg - Beloved Queen of Asgard

For anyone who seeks to connect with Frigg, whether just getting to know this powerful deity or seeking to delve deeper, Ryan McClain's book is a great resource. From the first literary mentions of Frigg to a modern day understanding of her, McClain takes the reader on a journey in which he uncovers every aspect of this deity. The book gives thorough consideration to both Germanic and Norse sources while beautifully weaving in the author's personal gnosis. Great scholarship and personal style blend in *Frigg - Beloved Queen of Asgard*, a book which stands out as both a homage to the goddess and a guide for those seeking her.

Daniela Simina, Author of *Where Fairies Meet: Parallels between Irish and Romanian Fairy Traditions*

McClain's *Frigg - Beloved Queen of Asgard* is a fascinating insight into this Nordic Goddess. A welcomed balance between historical fact and the author's own opinions and experiences, this book will suit those who appreciate a scholarly approach and those who enjoy learning from others' experiences. A great book for both beginners and those already familiar with this Goddess, there is much to be learned within the pages of McClain's well-written dedication to such an influential figure in Norse mythology.

Jessica Howard, Author of *The Art of Lithomancy* and *The Water Witch: An Introduction to Water Witchcraft*

T0002145

Ryan McClain sets in his book the base for a first approach to Frigg. If you follow the arrows he leaves for the seekers in these pages, I'm sure they will find enough to later go deeper in the right direction.

Ness Bosch

Pagan Portals

Frigg

Beloved Queen of Asgard

Pagan Portals

Frigg

Beloved Queen of Asgard

Ryan McClain

MOON
BOOKS
Winchester, UK
Washington, USA

JOHN HUNT PUBLISHING

First published by Moon Books, 2024
Moon Books is an imprint of John Hunt Publishing Ltd., No. 3 East Street, Alresford
Hampshire SO24 9EE, UK
office@jhpbooks.net
www.johnhuntpublishing.com
www.moon-books.net

For distributor details and how to order please visit the 'Ordering' section on our website.

Text copyright: Ryan McClain 2023

ISBN: 978 1 80341 370 9
978 1 80341 371 6 (ebook)
Library of Congress Control Number: 2022949989

A CIP catalogue record for this book is available from the British Library.

Design: Lapiz Digital Services

UK: Printed and bound by CPI Group (UK) Ltd, Croydon, CR0 4YY
Printed in North America by CPI GPS partners

We operate a distinctive and ethical publishing philosophy in all areas of our business, from our global network of authors to production and worldwide distribution.

Contents

Preface

My first book was all about connecting to the wilds of nature. It was the documentation of an outward spiritual experience where I discussed connecting with the world around me. The Gaulish Abnoba taught me how to pull from these experiences and knowledge to write a book. She then gave me the courage to submit it for publication. When it came time for choosing the topic of my second book it was obvious who it needed to be about. After all, Frigg has been a constant in my life longer than any other specific deity except, perhaps, for Mother Earth. Now that I gained a bit of confidence in my abilities Frigg began to nudge me into writing about her. This journey with Frigg has been an inward process of getting to know myself. It was about finding my personal role in life.

I must admit some initial hesitation in writing this book. After Abnoba I had locked myself into the identity as a Gaulish Polytheist, but that is only a part of who I am. I actually consider myself a multi-traditional polytheist. I feel that some frown on this as they see it as too eclectic. However, in the past it was quite common for people to adopt gods from other pantheons into their practices. The Romans were well known for doing this. In addition, my practice meanders quite often. I will honor a deity for several months before another one returns to me from some other area that requires additional work to be done. Frequently the deity will be from a different culture than the last one I was honoring. More often than not these gods and goddesses are from a Celtic or Germanic culture, but on occasion even Egyptian deities will pop in for a visit. In the end I decided to write what was true for my practice and admit my spiritual path is not so 'pure.'

Over the past several years, numerous books have come out dedicated to various gods. These books have had a level of scholarship that I feel had not been present in Paganism up to that point. It has been a joy to read many of these books, but I had not found one specifically geared towards Frigg. I have spent many years learning what I can about Frigg, and this book is a record of what I have gained in that process. It is the culmination of both lived and learned experiences. While it is not designed to be the one true source of what Frigg can offer, it is meant as a beginner's guide for those new to this journey.

It is my fervent hope that I did Frigg justice with this text. My goal is that I was able to put forth what I have learned and essentially repackage it into an easily discernable format. Frigg is a very down-to-earth goddess, and yet she has a no-nonsense attitude. She appreciates hard work and perseverance, but she recognizes when we at least put forth an effort. In the end, I feel that she would approve of this book for its purest intentions. I set out to offer the basics of what we know of her in one place, and I wanted to offer some practical methods for applying what was learned. Only time will tell how she feels about this text. I am sure she will let me know in her own way. Until then, may it serve you well on your path.

Finally, one last point I would like to drive home here is an unfortunate one that becomes increasingly necessary. There is a very vocal variety of Heathenry that seems to steal the spotlight quite often. They possess the very ugly face of racism and bigotry in its various manifestations. All religious traditions have these voices, but in Germanic Polytheism they tend to proliferate like an infection. The only way to confront this is not to run and hide from the label, but to make our voices louder. Heathenry is indeed a path for all. This book is for all that feel called to Frigg in her various roles, and whose hearts are free from hatred.

Acknowledgements

I wish to thank my husband for his constant support throughout the process of writing this book. Despite my doubts you make me believe in myself. I love you more.

I wish to thank my parents for being my biggest supporters and for always knowing I had this in me. I love you both.

I want to extend a thank you to my Aunt Judy. As far back as I have memories you have always believed in my worth. It has meant so much to me. Here is to many more years of Wednesday night chats!

Throughout the process of writing this book, and releasing the last one, I have learned a great deal about those near and dear to me. Of these people, my family has gone above and beyond to display their joy in my accomplishments. My family is obviously too large to list everyone, but to my brother and sister and their respective spouses and children, I thank you from the bottom of my heart.

Introduction

If you were to ask a group of Heathens to name a Norse goddess, chances are about half will mention the name Frigg. Her name is among the most well-known of the Æsir. Though not as popular as her husband, Odin, her stepson, Thor, or maybe even the goddess Freyja, many are familiar with her. Still, outside of the myth involving her son Baldr, some may come up empty handed recounting her stories. Unfortunately, this is a side effect of the little recorded lore involving all the goddesses of the Norse. However, there is still a lot that we can glean from the available sources to put together a solid framework that will help us in honoring Frigg.

For those that are unfamiliar with Frigg, you may be wondering who she is, and what roles she presides over. Frigg is first and foremost a goddess of the Æsir, one of the primary Norse families of gods (the other being the Vanir). She is, in fact, often regarded as their queen. Frigg is the wife of Odin, who is the All-Father of the Æsir. As the chief goddess of the Æsir she is sometimes known as the All-Mother. Together with Odin she is the infamous mother of the aforementioned Baldr, and the mother-in-law to Nanna. Frigg is also the stepmother to several gods; such as Thor. She is the daughter of the mysterious Fjörgynn. Frigg is also the possessor of a falcon-feathered cloak, and she resides in the marshy halls of Fensalir.

From the earliest attested story, *Origin of the Tribe of the Lombards*, to the Scandinavian sagas hundreds of years later, Frigg shows herself to be a multifaceted goddess. Her importance cannot be discounted. As we will learn, these ancient Germanic people designated Friday as her special day. In the Roman calendar this day was sacred to the Goddess Venus. Interestingly, they also connected Frigg to the planet Venus, called 'Frigg's Star' in Old Norse. Venus was not the only celestial body dedicated to Frigg, as Orion's belt was called 'Frigg's Spindle' or some variation thereof. These are each strong pieces of evidence for the worship of Frigg, and her high place among these ancient societies.

The gods, on at least one occasion, are referred to collectively as *Friggjar niðjar* or 'descendants of Frigg' lending further attestation to her importance (Grundy, 2002, p. 56). This is probably a symbolic title as Baldr is her only known son by birth. However, I see Frigg giving her love to all her stepsons as if they belong to her and Odin alone. Odin himself is even given the kenning of 'Dweller in Frigg's embrace' showing her place of prominence in his life (Haraldskvæði). She is quite often defined by these relationships. In fact, a known kenning for Frigg is 'Co-Wife of Jörd and Rindr and Gunnlöd and Grídr' linking her to these beings simply from their association as lovers of Odin. These relationships with other gods do form a strong part of her identity, but she is so much more than this.

Frigg is a goddess who holds sway over many aspects. Some of them are closely related, yet others are distinctly different. She is at once the 'All-Mother' and 'Goddess of Marriage', but she is also the 'Peace-Keeper' and 'Goddess of Fate'. She is a goddess who oversees matters of love in all its forms. In fact, the root of her name is thought to mean 'beloved one' springing from the Proto-Germanic *frijjō*. The myths bear this connection with love out in numerous ways. From the love that she has for Odin, who has many times stepped outside of their marriage, to the love for her son Baldr, who she loses so tragically.

Frigg is a wise goddess who often outwits her equally matched husband. On at least two occasions we will see them face off with each other, and Frigg holds her own both times. Frigg is a goddess of healing, as we will see in at least one instance, where she works charms to heal a horse. As a goddess of the hearth and home she is goddess of domestic crafts in all its varied forms. She is the ever-mourning mother of Baldr, and a goddess of great strength when faced with that very loss. Frigg knows the fates of all, yet she never speaks of them. Indeed, a heavy burden to bear.

As the Queen of the Æsir she leads a host of Asynjur, or goddesses. As we will establish, many people view them as her royal court, or her handmaidens. Whether these are mere hypostases of Frigg, entirely separate goddesses, or something in between will be up to the reader to decide. Some of them, such as Gefjun and Fulla participate quite independently in the myths. However, some, such as Hlín, may be a byname used for Frigg on at least one occasion. Whatever you do, do not let the term 'handmaiden' dissuade you from giving them reverence. These are powerful entities in their own right, and they deserve our respect.

Frigg is a goddess of great complexity, that I sincerely hope I illustrate with the following text. I will begin in the first two chapters by analyzing the various myths that she takes part in. In the third chapter I undertake a further examination of the roles and symbols that are attached to Frigg. The next chapter highlights those that are considered relatives of Frigg. The notable exception being a discussion on the goddesses Freyja and her relationship with Frigg. I felt that this was a topic that needed to be discussed somewhere in the book and that spot seemed most appropriate. The fifth chapter will be the one dedicated to those goddesses most connected with Frigg. They are the ones previously referred to as her handmaidens. They serve crucial functions in my work with Frigg, and I felt them worthy of their own chapter. In the final chapter we will discuss such things as altars, offerings, prayers, and holy days.

This book is not intended to be the one final say on Frigg. As the subject of Frigg is not often the source of such texts, I felt this was an important one to write. It is an introductory book for those either just starting out on their journey with Frigg or wishing to compliment it. I have tried to make it a one stop location for the sources where she is mentioned. The references at the back of the book serve to expand on what is discussed here. I recommend these titles, and hope that this is only the beginning of your path. Frigg has a great deal of wisdom that she can impart on the world today. So, sit back and enjoy this exploration of Frigg: Beloved Queen of Asgard.

Chapter 1

Frigg in the Early Sources

Frigg comes to us from a variety of sources and through different eras of time. In this chapter I will be discussing Frigg as she appears in the lore from the earliest recorded periods. First, I will take a brief glimpse at her earliest attestations, such as possible place name evidence that we have available. While it is mostly speculative, it can offer us some insight. Next, I will look at Frigg in the early southern Germanic record by examining the *Origin of the Lombards* and the *Second Merseburg Incantation*. While this is not a great deal of material, it does offer us some crucial tidbits of information that help to define her roles. I will follow this up with a discussion on the *History of the Danes* by Saxo Grammaticus. The works of Saxo would normally be grouped with the Scandinavian sources that follow in the next chapter. However, because they were composed just a bit earlier and offer a differing viewpoint, I have included them in this chapter. Hopefully, together this will provide an interesting picture of how Frigg was viewed by these earlier societies before taking a more thorough look at the Scandinavian Edda's and sagas in the following chapter.

These works are very important for us to get an idea of how Frigg was seen in the past. They provide us with a glimpse at her roles and attributes which can give us ideas on how we can work with her today. It is important to keep in mind that much of the information that follows was recorded by Christian authors. While this does not make the information obsolete it is important to recognize because it can cloud the notions that are commonly held about Frigg. For instance, Saxo seems to frame the gods as mere wizards who accomplish great deeds.

Still, these remain important sources in getting to know Frigg, as well as other deities.

Another thing to keep in mind is that Frigg will appear under a variety of names between cultures. The Germanic people were not a monolith, but an array of diverse groups united by common linguistic origins and closely related religious beliefs. There exist different schools of thought regarding the variety of names that will be presented here. On the one hand, we have those that believe each cultural depiction of Frigg, under these various names, is a unique goddess unto herself, and as such, worthy of individual veneration. On the other hand, we have those that feel that all these goddesses are identical but are known under different spellings. For the purposes of this book, they will be discussed as one goddess, but how you choose to view them is entirely your choice.

Etymology

I thought I would start with deciphering the name Frigg. A name can tell you a lot about someone, and this is no different when it concerns the divine. It is believed that Frigg was known throughout the Germanic world under various spellings of her name. She is, of course, Frigg in Scandinavia, and named Frigga in the Danish historian Saxo's work. Frigga is also a common Anglicization of her name as well. She is also called Frea in the *Origin of the Tribe of the Lombards*, and Frija in the *Second Merseburg Incantation* which are both southern continental sources. Both do have superficial similarities with Freyja, but they are indeed the early Germanic forms of the Scandinavian Frigg. Finally, she was known by both Frige and Fricg among the Anglo-Saxon's. The name itself is believed to be derived from Proto-Germanic *frijjō* meaning something along the lines of "beloved one, wife" (Asdisardottir, 2005, p. 420). This would make it cognate with the Sanskrit *priya* also meaning "beloved one" (Simek, 2007, p. 94).

Early Attestations and Place Names

The earliest attestation of Frigg comes in the form of the Old High German Friatag and Old English Frigedeag. These are the early forms of the weekday now commonly referred to as Freitag in modern German and Friday in modern English. It is estimated that the names of these days were in use by at least the 4th century CE (Simek, 2007). This day was dedicated to Venus in the Roman calendar. This could lend to the identification of Frigg with the role of love and beauty, or it exists because this idea was already held by these people. Writing in around 1000 CE, Ælfric of Eynsham identifies Frigg with Venus as well. He states: "the shameless goddess called Venus and Frigg in Danish" (Näsström, 1995, p. 109). It is interesting that he uses the Old Norse form Frigg instead of the Old English Frige. This shows the level of influence that the Scandinavians had at the time of his writing.

There may be additional evidence of the worship of Frigg in England. This exists on the toponymic record as there may be some places that were initially named for her. Herbert (2010) cites several of these. Among those she names are Friden in Derbyshire, which may have meant "Valley of Frige," and would have originally been called Frigeden. There is Fretherne, originally Frithorn, which could mean "Thorn-tree of Frige" in Gloucestershire. Finally, from Hampshire there is both Freefolk, originally Frigefolc, and Froyle, originally Freohyll, each meaning "People of Frige" and "Hill of Frige" respectively. It must be stated though that the connection between these places and Frigg is only speculation.

In Sweden there may be additional lands dedicated to Frigg. There are two locations there that were referred to as Friggjarakr, meaning "Frigg's Cornfield," in Västergötland (Turville-Petre, 1964). There is also a Fristad in Östergötland that may be named for Frigg as well (Ingham, 1985). Additionally, there was at one point a Friggjarsetr in Hegra, Norway, as the name of a farm that

11

has since been lost (Ross et al., 2007). Ingham also references the towns of Friggaskulle and Friggesthorp, but she also points out that these are of a more modern origin and illustrates little of ancient pagan cultic practice. Still, it is worthy to note them as Frigg obviously held a place of prominence among these people even into later times. It is due in part to all these aforementioned locations that a link to land fertility and Frigg may be construed.

In addition to these place names, Grimm (1882) states that among the Swedes Orion's Belt is known as *Friggerock*, which means 'Frigg's Spindle' (p. 302). Näsström (1995) reports the name as either *Friggerocken* or *Friggetenen*, and translates it as "the spinning wheel of Frigg" (p. 110). I have also seen this translated a few times as "Frigg's Distaff". At any rate, we can see a link to spinning and Frigg from this example. Finally, Ingham (1985) mentions that the planet Venus was called Friggjarstjarna, meaning "Frigg's Star" in Old Norse (p. 123). This coincides well with Frigg's connection to Venus from the day of the week. Plants were also named in honor of Frigg. Grimm goes on to name hionagras, a type of orchid-*Orchis maculata*, as "Friggjargras" (p. 304). This flower was apparently used to make a love potion. Once again this serves to support a link with Venus.

Origin of the Tribe of the Lombards

The first time that Frigg enters the historical record through the lore is in the 7th century *Origo Gentis Langobardorum*, or the *Origin of the Tribe of the Longobards*. The Longobards are known more commonly under spelling Lombards. Paul the Deacon would later derive his 8th century work *History of the Langobards* from this account. In this tale Frigg is known under the spelling of Frea and Odin under the name of Godan. The Winniles in this tale are commonly believed to be the Germanic tribe known as the Vandals. The story as told by Paul goes as follows:

There is an island that is called Scadanan, which is interpreted "destruction," in the regions of the north, where many people dwell. Among these there was a small people that was called the Winniles. And with them was a woman, Gambara by name, and she had two sons. Ybor was the name of one and Agio the name of the other. They, with their mother, Gambara by name, held the sovereignty over the Winniles. Then the leaders of the Wandals, that is, Ambri and Assi, moved with their army, and said to the Winniles: 'Either pay us tribute or prepare yourselves for battle and fight with us.' Then answered Ybor and Agio, with their mother Gambara: 'It is better for us to make ready the battle than to pay tributes to the Wandals.' Then Ambri and Assi, that is, the leaders of the Wandals, asked Godan that he should give them the victory over the Winniles. Godan answered, saying: 'Whom I shall first see when at sunrise, to them will I give the victory.' At that time Gambara with her two sons, that is, Ybor and Agio, who were chiefs over the Winniles, besought Frea, the wife of Godan, to be propitious to the Winniles. Then Frea gave counsel that at sunrise the Winniles should come, and that their women, with their hair let down around the face in the likeness of a beard, should also come with their husbands. Then when it became bright, while the sun was rising, Frea, the wife of Godan, turned around the bed where her husband was lying and put his face towards the east and awakened him. And he, looking at then, saw the Winniles and their women having their hair let down around the face. And he says, 'Who are these Long-beards?' And Frea said to Godan, 'As you have given them a name, give them also the victory.' And he gave them the victory, so that they should defend themselves according to his counsel and obtain the victory. From that time the Winniles were called Langobards (Translated by Foulke, W. D., 1907).

This story is quite telling where it regards Frigg. She is a very cunning goddess. She can outmaneuver her husband who is frequently believed to be among the wisest of the gods. I find it particularly fascinating that she even thought of the minute details such as positioning the bed to face the correct direction. She genuinely thought of everything to see to it that she, and the Lombards, came out victorious in this situation over her husband and the Wandals (Vandals). We will learn later that this is not the only occasion of Frigg going head-to-head with Odin. This early attestation to their dynamic relationship makes this one of my favorite myths involving Frigg. I would argue that it is also one of the most impressive as it concerns the significant role that Frigg initially played among the early Germanic people. In this tale, she is on equal footing with Odin according to these ancient Germanic groups.

Second Merseburg Incantation

The Merseburg Incantations are two charms that were discovered in 1841 by Georg Waitz in a theological manuscript in Fulda, Germany. The precise dating of the incantations is not known, but they are believed to date to around the 10th century (Simek, 2007). Both charms are important clues to the past spiritual beliefs of these peoples. However, it is the second charm that is of particular importance as it is the primary continental source for the names of several deities. The charm reads as follows:

Phol and Wodan went to [the] woods
now Balder's foal wrenched its foot
Sinthgunt charmed it, Sunna's sister,
Frija charmed it, Volla's sister,
Woden charmed it as he well could,
as bone-wrench, so blood-wrench,
so limb-wrench,
bone to bone, blood to blood,
limb to limb, so they may be joined
(Translated by Pollington, S., 2011)

14

Immediately identifiable is Odin, here called Wodan. He appears to be leading this particular outing. Frija is none other than the Old High German form of Frigg. Additionally, Volla is believed to be Fulla of the Norse sources. Interestingly, she is listed here as a sister to Frigg, but in Scandinavian literature she is the chief handmaiden to Frigg. This would explain their close relationship in the later lore. Whether this sisterly bond was intended to be literal or metaphorical in this text may never be known. I will discuss Fulla in further detail in Chapter 5.

Regarding Balder, he is typically thought to be Baldr, but this may simply be a title referencing Wodan or Phol as 'lord'. As to the identity of Phol numerous theories abound. The most common conclusion being that he is one and the same as Baldr. However, others suggest the possibility that he may be a counterpart/partner of Volla (Pollington, 2011 and Simek, 2007). In this analogy it would be Fol/Vol and Fulla/Volla. Simek even mentions a possible correspondence between these two and Freyr and Freyja. If this is the case, we have an amazing example of all the power players in the Norse myths interacting in German sources. Save for Thor, nearly all the primary deities would be involved. Sunna is the Old High German form for Sol of Norse lore, making her the sun goddess.

Finally, the exact function of Sinthgunt has confounded scholars. In the original manuscript Sinthgunt is actually spelled as *Sinhtgunt*. This would lead to a translation as 'the night-walking one' and could reference the moon (Simek, 2007). As she is a sister with Sunna, the sun, this makes a degree of sense. However, the moon is typically seen as male in Germanic beliefs. If the correct spelling is to be Sinthgunt, then various other interpretations are available. Simek mentions a couple of other explanations such as; "the one moving into battle" and "heavenly body, star" as put forth by other scholars on the subject (p. 285).

As for Frigg, we learn here that in addition to having a sister she is a healer who sings healing charms as well. This is not something we see in Norse mythology where Frigg is concerned so it is an interesting discovery. Her sister, Volla, apparently possesses the same ability. Though the text makes it difficult to determine if Volla and Sunna are present, or if they are merely placed in the text for poetic purposes.

If Balder is taken to be Baldr, the son of Frigg and Odin, then this is an intriguing little family outing. The various deities depicted has led to much speculation as to their identities. This would also be the first occurrence of Frigg appearing as a mother figure in the lore. As we will learn in the following chapter, Frigg makes helping Baldr a priority in her life. Not at all surprising given a mother's love for her child.

History of the Danes

Gesta Danorum, or the *History of the Danes*, was composed in the late 12th and early 13th centuries by the Danish historian Saxo Grammaticus. This piece discusses the history of the Danish peoples from prehistory on through the 12th century. His works have not received the notoriety of the Eddas, but it is still an important text. In the following passage we see a side to Frigg that one may think seems more compatible with the stories of Freya. It does not necessarily depict Frigg in what many would consider a favorable light, but this may be due to prejudices that Saxo had regarding all the deities he discusses. In fact, Saxo seems to imagine the gods as mortals of great power and magic. Overall, I feel that these writings are much drier and cynical than the notions we typically have of the deities. This excerpt is the primary one concerning Frigg, here called Frigga, and it reads as follows:

At this time there was one Odin, who was credited over all Europe with the honour, which was false, of godhead, but used more continually to sojourn at Upsala; and in this spot, either from the sloth of the inhabitants or from its own pleasantness, he vouchsafed to dwell with somewhat especial constancy. The kings of the North, desiring more zealously to worship his deity, embounded his likeness in a golden image; and this statue, which betokened their homage, they transmitted with much show of worship to Byzantium, fettering even the effigied arms with a serried mass of bracelets. Odin was overjoyed at such notoriety, and greeted warmly the devotion of the senders. But his queen Frigga, desiring to go forth more beautified, called smiths, and had the gold stripped from the statue. Odin hanged them, and mounted the statue upon a pedestal, which by the marvellous skill of his art he made to speak when a mortal touched it. But still Frigga preferred the splendour of her own apparel to the divine honours of her husband, and submitted herself to the embraces of one of her servants; and it was by this man's device she broke down the image, and turned to the service of her private wantonness that gold which had been devoted to public idolatry. Little thought she of practicing unchastity, that she might the easier satisfy her greed, this woman so unworthy to be the consort of a god; but what should I here add, save that such a godhead was worthy of such a wife? So great was the error that of old befooled the minds of men. Thus Odin, wounded by the double trespass of his wife, resented the outrage to his image as keenly as that to his bed; and, ruffled by these two stinging dishonours, took to an exile overflowing with noble shame, imagining so to wipe off the slur of his ignominy (Elton, O., 1905).

As we can see, Frigg is more concerned here with gold than over any other matter. She apparently embarrasses her husband, Odin, to the point of self-exile. This flies in the face of the typical image of the chaste housewife many seem to place on her. I do feel that Saxo seems to have something against Frigg as this is so far out of the scope of her usual character. However, Odin is quite commonly depicted having extramarital affairs with numerous other beings. Frigg simply had desires that she took it upon herself to fulfill. The idea that Odin was so embarrassed that he had to self-exile seems a bit on the dramatic side for him. Again, I feel this is due to Saxo and his devout religious leanings clouding his writing. However, the importance of this unique take on Frigg cannot be overlooked.

Personal Take

These earliest sources for Frigg, while sparse in number, are quite informative. We learn of a side to her here that we will not see in later chapters. First, the meaning of her name, and her connection to the day of the week Friday, tell us quite a bit. She is immediately recognizable as a goddess of love. When it comes to Frigg this cannot be passed off blithely. I thank Frigg for bringing love into my life at a point when I was resigned to live it in solitude. There has been a joy to my existence ever since.

Next, in the story about the Lombards, her quick wit and cunning is on full display. She appears as a very skilled adversary, and I do not think that her dominant role in this tale can be overstated. We will witness the Eddas and great sagas of Scandinavia in the next chapter, and the high level of respect placed on the gods, Odin in particular. That is why it is even more astounding when one considers that Frigg was able to get the best of Odin. She must have been truly well respected by the people for them to have recorded her playing that part.

In the *Second Merseburg Incantation* we discussed her brief role, but it is important to look at it again. Here she participates in healing magic. This is a genuine display of her divine powers. Holistic health is an endeavor that I personally feel has a strong link to Frigg, and it is in no small part because of this charm. The healing powers of herbs, spices, and plants in general should be prized far more heavily than it is. Together, with prayer to Frigg, it is a powerful combination not to be taken lightly.

Lastly, the role she plays in the *History of the Danes* is to be considered. Here is a story that many, especially those of that time period, would have frowned upon. I do not see the story of a wife stepping out on her husband. Truth be told, this is a story of a woman going after what she wants in the exact manner that we will see Odin do in later myths. Two wrongs may not make a right, but who are we to determine the intricacies of another's marriage; let alone the marriage of two gods.

All told, we have already learned more about Frigg than the common person will ever discover in a cursory search of her. These early legends are a testament to the power of love, healing, and personal desires of the chief goddess of the Æsir. These ancient people probably revered Frigg for her personal sovereignty, and she deserves that respect today. The image we are developing of Frigg will become even more full in the following chapters, but I hope that this served as a great introduction to the queen herself.

Chapter 2

Frigg in the Norse Record

In this chapter I will look to the Eddas and sagas of Scandinavian literature. This is where the bulk of the information on the Germanic deities come from, and that is no different for Frigg. It is for this reason that I have chosen to discuss them here in a separate chapter. These sources were recorded by Christian writers which does skew the view of the gods somewhat. For instance, Snorri Sturluson, composer of the *Prose Edda*, initially relates that the gods are from Troy in modern day Turkey that just happen to possess great skills. Despite this, these written accounts provide a nice background on Frigg, and they offer some clues as to her worship.

While there is a great deal of information and stories of the Norse gods, the goddesses did not fare as well by the writers that recorded their tales. Some may assume, and maybe correctly, that the goddesses did not hold as much importance as the gods once did. However, it is also possible that this is because the people that recorded the stories were male themselves who were relaying stories passed down through a warrior class. It may be due to the fact that the functions of the goddesses did not correlate to epic tales in the way that the gods did. There could be other reasons, or maybe it is a combination of each of these, but it is what it is. In the case of Frigg, we are fortunate in that she did play a more prominent role than most other goddesses did. In fact, other than Freyja, one could argue that Frigg was the most highly revered and written about of the goddesses.

Poetic Edda

The *Poetic Edda* was composed in the 13th century, but it is believed to be derived from much older source material. Frigg receives several mentions in the *Poetic Edda* including in *Völuspá*, *Vafþrúðnismál*, *Grímnismál*, *Lokasenna*, and *Oddrúnargrátr*. I will recount these references to Frigg here, but I must note that the particular stanza mentioned will vary from source to source depending on the translator. At the most, any given translation should only be off by one or two stanzas.

Völuspá

In *Völuspá*, which roughly translates to "The Witch's Prophecy" in English, the events of Ragnarok are foretold. Frigg is referenced twice specifically, and perhaps a third time, in this poem. In stanza 34 it is stated that: "But in Fensalir / did Frigg weep sore / For Valhall's need: / would you know yet more?" (Bellows, 1936, p. 15). This passage is in reference to her most notorious tale; that of the death of her son Baldr. Following this, Frigg is referenced in stanza 53: "Now comes to Hlín / yet another hurt, / When Othin fares / to fight with the wolf, / And Beli's fair slayer / seeks out Surt, / For there must fall / the joy of Frigg" (Bellows, 1936, p. 22). We can see from both excerpts that Frigg has endured much hardship. This bears witness to the inherent strength that she possesses. In the line that states, "Now comes to Hlín" it is common for many translators to substitute Frigg's name for that of Hlín. It is typically assumed, due to the reference to Odin, that in this instance Hlín is simply a byname of Frigg. Hlín will be discussed further in Chapter 5.

Vafþrúðnismál

In the beginning of *Vafþrúðnismál*, Frigg partakes in a conversation with Odin. Odin asks Frigg whether he should go and speak with the wise and powerful jotunn Vafþruðnir; meaning Riddle-Weaver in English. Frigg advises Odin not to go, but Odin is insistent. Frigg then tells Odin to travel and be safe on his journey before Odin finally takes his leave. It appears Odin has already made his decision to take on this journey, but he is still in need of Frigg's approval before his departure. It is interesting that this great god of wisdom still seeks out the counsel of his wife. Perhaps this is due, in part, to Frigg's ability of foreknowledge. If it is, then it is curious that Odin ignores her initial advice. However, it could be nothing more than the normal concern a wife would have for her husband who was about to go on a dangerous journey.

Grímnismál

Frigg plays an important part in *Grímnismál* though she is only discussed in the introduction. This tale involves the two sons of King Hrauthung. There was Agnar, who was ten years old, and Geirroth, who was eight. The two sons took a boat out to catch some fish, but the wind took them out to sea. They eventually wrecked onto land one night and met a poor farmer there. The two boys then spent the winter with this old farmer and his wife. The farmer would go on to foster Geirroth while his wife fostered Agnar. The farmer and his wife are really Odin and Frigg in disguise. When spring finally came around the farmer gave the boys a boat, but before they left the farmer spoke privately with Geirroth.

The two boys departed. When they finally arrived back at their father's shore Geirroth quickly got up and jumped on land. Then Geirroth shoved the boat back out to sea and shouted: "Go wherever the trolls take you!" (Crawford, 2015, p. 60). As the boat drifted away Geirroth proceeded to his father's hall. Upon arriving, Geirroth learned that his father had died, and now he was to become king.

Odin and Frigg watched this from their seat, Hlithskjalf. Here they were able to see all the worlds. Odin taunted Frigg by saying that her foster son, Agnar, fathers' children with a troll, but Geirroth is a king. Frigg responds that Odin's foster son Geirroth is stingy and mistreats his guests. Odin does not believe this, and so he makes a bet with Frigg over the matter.

Meanwhile, Frigg sends her handmaiden Fulla down to Geirroth to warn him that a wizard will be arriving. Fulla tells Geirroth that he will know this man because no dog will attack him. In response Geirroth orders that if a man comes that no dog will attack, he is to be captured. When Odin finally does arrive, dressed in a blue cape and calling himself Grimnir, he is quickly apprehended. Then Geirroth proceeds to have him tortured and placed between two fires. He was kept there for eight nights.

King Geirroth had a ten-year-old son named Agnar, named after his uncle. The boy felt his father had mistreated Grimnir and he offered him a horn to drink from. In the meantime, the fire had begun to burn Grimnir's back. Grimnir finally identifies himself to the boy as Odin, and thanks him for the proper hospitality. Odin goes on to tell Agnar about various things such as the halls of the gods.

Frigg is not mentioned further, but the story does go on to relay how King Geirroth discovers who Grimnir is himself. After he finds out he wishes to remove Odin from the flames, but he trips and falls on his sword killing himself. At this point Odin leaves and Agnar is crowned king, and he reigns for many prosperous years.

This is another one of my favorite stories involving Frigg. First, I find it so interesting in part because of the roles Frigg and Odin play in the beginning as a farmer and his wife. Second, once again, Frigg takes on Odin. While it may at first appear that Odin wins in this instance by getting Geirroth into position to be king, I feel that it is Frigg that comes out on top. It is the kindly young Agnar, namesake of his uncle, who is a successful king. Geirroth, even if by deception, wound up to be a poor ruler. Frigg manipulated the situation just as Odin did by whispering in the young Geirroth's ear. One could rightly assume that the implication is that Odin told Geirroth to shove his brother out to sea. While neither one exactly played fair, Frigg still seems to have won out in the end.

Lokasenna

In *Lokasenna*, which essentially means "Loki's Taunts" in English, Frigg has a few stanzas where she speaks with Loki amidst his insults. It all goes down in the hall of the god Aegir. The insults that Loki projects on the others are sometimes humorous, and at other times quite cruel. The interaction with Frigg is particularly mean-spirited.

Frigg tells Loki that he should not be repeating everyone's history, and that the past belongs in the past. Loki responds that Frigg needs to be quiet. He reveals that she is Fjörgynn's daughter, and that Frigg has slept with Odin's brothers Vili and Ve in the past. Frigg tells Loki that if Baldr were present he would not speak to her in that manner, and that he would be killed if he did. Loki says that he is the one that made it so that Baldr would never come home. Then Freyja interjects telling Loki he is crazy for taunting Frigg as she knows the fate of everyone, even if she never reveals what she knows.

It is apparent in this exchange that the events took place after the death of Baldr. This makes Loki's remarks pointedly vicious. We also hear from Freyja of Frigg's clairvoyant abilities. It is also interesting that we see Frigg and Freyja in the same scene interacting with each other. *Lokasenna* is believed to be a later addition to the *Poetic Edda*. Simek (2007) states that it was likely composed in the 12th century. However, Grundy (2002) points out that the language and meter could suggest an early date for *Lokasenna*.

Oddrúnargrátr

Finally, Frigg's name is invoked in *Oddrúnargrátr*. This is also another instance where Frigg and Freyja are referenced together. This story involves a woman named Borgny, who was the daughter of a king named Heithrek. She was about to give birth and needed help when Oddrun, sister of Brynhild and Attila, arrives. Oddrun sang powerful spells at Borgny's side before she finally gave birth to a boy and a girl. When Borgny is finally able to speak, she says: "So may the holy / ones thee help, / Frigg and Freyja / and favoring gods, / As thou hast saved me / from sorrow now" (Bellows, 1936, p. 472). The story does continue from there with Oddrun recounting her tragic love affair with the man named Gunnar.

This is a rare case that we get to witness an actual prayer to Frigg, as well as Freyja. In this case, they both appear as patronesses of childbirth in a sense. Crawford (2015) does state that this poem, "…was probably composed fairly late" (p. 319). Grundy (2002) seems to agree when he says, "This poem, however, is often thought to be among the youngest of the Eddic lays" (p. 60). The author obviously envisioned Frigg and Freyja as separate goddesses just as was displayed in *Lokasenna*, but this will be discussed further in Chapter 4.

Prose Edda

The *Prose Edda* was written in the 13th century by the poet and historian Snorri Sturluson. It differs from the *Poetic Edda* in that it has a single author. In the *Prose Edda*, Frigg is referenced on several occasions. She is first mentioned in the Prologue where it discusses the lineage of Odin. Here, in section three, Sturluson records: "His wife was Frígídá, whom we call Frigg" (Sturluson & Brodeur, 1916, p. 7). He continues in section four stating: "Odin had second sight, and his wife also; and from their foreknowledge he found that his name should be exalted in the northern part of the world and glorified above the fame of all other kings" (p. 7).

Gylfaginning

In *Gylfaginning* 9 we again hear of Frigg and Odin and their high status. When discussing Asgard, which Sturluson calls Troy, he states: "When Odin sat in its high seat, he could see through all worlds and into all men's doings. Moreover, he understood everything he saw. His wife was called Frigg, Fjörgyn's daughter, and from this family has come the kindred we call the family of the Æsir. They lived in Old Asgard and the realms that belong to it; each member of this family is divine" (p. 18).

Gylfaginning 20 discusses Odin as the All-Father. It relates that he is the highest god and that the other gods look to him as a father. Then we are told: "Frigg is his wife, and she knows all the fates of men, though she speaks no prophecy" (Sturluson & Brodeur, 1916, p. 33). After this, the section from the *Poetic Edda* where Loki is called out is referenced: "Thou art mad now, / Loki, and reft of mind, / Why, Loki, leav'st thou not off? / Frigg, methinks, / is wise in all fates, / Though herself say them not!" (p. 33). The *Poetic Edda* asserts that this last stanza is said by Freyja, but in the *Prose Edda*, it is said that Odin speaks those words.

Next, we see mention of Frigg in *Gylfaginning* 35. The heading of this section is called 'Goddesses' and it provides several names of the Asynjur – the word Asynjur itself essentially means goddesses and Asynja means goddess. I will go over this section thoroughly in Chapter 5. However, I will highlight here where Frigg is mentioned. She is said to be the highest of the gods and resides in the hall, Fensalir; which translates as "Marsh Halls" (Simek, 2007).

Perhaps the most famous tale involving Frigg is found in *Gylfaginning* 49. Here, Frigg receives oaths not to cause harm to Baldr from: "... fire and water should spare Baldr, likewise iron and metal of all kinds, stones, earth, trees, sicknesses, beasts, birds, venom, serpents" (Sturluson & Brodeur, 1916, p. 71). This indicates the true power of Frigg as she can command vows from everything in the known world. Meanwhile the gods, thinking Baldr cannot be harmed, commence shooting at him. Loki becomes angry by this and transforms himself into a woman and ventures to Fensalir to see Frigg.

Once Loki has arrived at Fensalir, he makes inquiries about the oaths made and questions if everything truly swore one to her. Frigg responds: "There grows a tree-sprout alone westward of Valhall: it is called Mistletoe; I thought it too young to ask the oath of" (Sturluson & Brodeur, 1916, p. 71). Loki takes his leave to fetch the mistletoe. He returns to Baldr and then proceeds to guide the hand of the blind god Hodr at shooting, and thus instantly killing, Baldr.

The gods are all overcome with anguish. Once the gods have all gained their composure, Frigg asks who will ride to Hel to offer a ransom so that Baldr may be returned. The god Hermod agrees to go. Upon arrival, the goddess Hel tells Hermod that if everyone weeps for Baldr then the god may be returned to them. Once Hermod returns, the gods set about the world asking for everything to weep for Baldr, and they do. They all weep that is except for the jotunn, Thokk, who is believed to be Loki in disguise once again. So Baldr was unable to return. This would be one of the great sorrows of Frigg's life.

Skáldskaparmál

Skáldskaparmál begins with the god Bragi relating stories to the god Aegir during a feast held by the Æsir. There were twelve gods in attendance and eight goddesses. Among the goddesses was Frigg, as well as Gefjun and Fulla. In addition, Freyja, Idunn, Gerd, Sigyn, and Nanna were there.

Later, in Skáldskaparmál 6, the gods venture out to a feast, this time hosted by Aegir. The gods that went included Odin, Njord, Freyr, Tyr, Bragi, Vidar, and Loki. The goddesses attending this feast included Frigg, Freyja, Gefjun, Skadi, Idunn, and Sif.

In *Skáldskaparmál* 4, *Thor Journeys to Geirrod's Courts*, we do not have any direct action on the part of Frigg, but her hawk cloak is referenced. The tale involves Loki going to spy on Geirrod. All we are told is: "This was because of what happened to Loki earlier when, in order to amuse himself, he put on Frigg's falcon shape, and the, driven by curiosity, he flew into Geirrod's courts" (Sturluson & Byock, 2005). Loki is, of course, caught and the story proceeds from there. However, it is interesting to see Frigg and her falcon/hawk form referenced and taking part in an actual myth.

The next section that we hear of Frigg in *Skáldskaparmál* is in the poetic references section. First, in the kennings, or compound bynames, for Odin section we are told that he is known as 'Dweller in Frigg's bosom' (Sturluson & Brodeur, 1916, p. 99). Further on, we are told that Baldr can be called 'Son of Odin and Frigg' and that Vali is called the 'Stepson of Frigg' (pp. 111 & 114). Next, in the same translation, under the section for Frigg we are given several kennings. These are read as follows: "Call her Daughter of Fjörgynn, Wife of Odin, Mother of Baldr, Co-Wife of Jörd and Rindr and Gunnlöd and Grídr, Mother-in-law of Nanna, Lady of the Æsir and Asynjur, Mistress of Fulla and of the Hawk-Plumage and of Fensalir" (p. 129).

Finally, the last part of *Skáldskaparmál* is commonly referred to as the *Nafnaþulur*. This section contains a list of 28 Asynjur and 9 Valkyries. The list of these figures reads as follows:

Now shall all the Asynjur be named. Frigg and Freyja, Fulla and Snotra, Gerd and Gefjun, Gná, Lofn, Skadi, Jörd and Idunn, Ilm, Bil, Njorun. Hlín and Nanna, Hnoss, Rind and Sjöfn, Sol and Sága, Sigyn and Vör. Then there is Vár and Syn must be named, but Thrud and Ran reckoned next to them.

Freyja also wept gold for Od. Her names are Horn, Thrunva, Syr, Skjalf and Gefn, and likewise Mardoll. Her daughters are Hnoss and Gersemi.

There are yet others, Odin's maids, Hild and Gondul, Hlokk, Mist,
Skogul. Then are listed Hrund and Eir, Hrist, Skuld. They are
called norns who shape necessity (Sturluson & Faulkes, 1998).

Several of these Asynjur will be covered in Chapter 5. A few
of them are scarcely mentioned outside of this list. The section
that refers to 'Odin's maids' is a term for Valkyries however the
sentence that follows seems to imply they may be Norns. One
of these, Eir, will be discussed in Chapter 5 as well. The last
name, Skuld, is one of the three Norns, but she is also listed as
a Valkyrie in *Gylfaginning* 36. I feel that this implies a strong
link between the Norns and Valkyries. After all, the Valkyries
do choose who is to die in battle and who will have victory; in
essence determining the fate of the warriors.

This sums up the majority, if not the totality, of references
in the *Poetic Edda* and *Prose Edda* to Frigg. That said, this is not
the only information available from Scandinavian sources. A
few of the sagas offer brief mentions of Frigg as well. In the
next section I will highlight a few of these short but intriguing
instances.

Sagas

Ynglinga Saga

In the 13th century *Heimskringla* Sturluson includes the *Ynglinga*
Saga. There exists only a brief mention of Frigg, but it is an
interesting tidbit. The third section of this saga involves the
two brothers of the god, Odin. These three together were the
first-born gods according to the creation myth in *Gylfaginning*
(Sturluson & Byock, 2005). They were the sons of Borr and the
jotunn Bestla. One brother is named Vili, which means "will" in
Old Norse, and the other brother is known as Ve, which means
"shrine" in Old Norse (Simek, 2007).

When Odin was wandering these two brothers would rule in
his stead. On one occasion Odin was away for a period so long

that people began to doubt his return. It is because of this that his brothers divided Odin's estate between them. However, it is stated that, "...both of them took his wife Frigg for themselves" (Sturluson & Laing, 1844). It came one day that Odin did return, and he then resumed his place next to Frigg.

This is the story that Loki seems to reference in *Lokasenna*. While this certainly can sound like a strange occurrence, there may be another explanation of these events. It is possible that in this story Frigg acts as a goddess of sovereignty. This would explain Vili and Ve having to share her. Their right to rule was not legitimate until they united with Frigg. Her approval would thus give them the divine right to rule. As she is wed to Odin, his return would signify the end of their reign as Frigg is dedicated to Odin. An additional theory is that Vili and Ve are simply aspects, or emanations, of Odin himself. Vili and Ve could be named aspects, or spiritual manifestations, of Odin. If this is the case Frigg was merely sleeping with Odin in his alternate forms.

Völsunga Saga

The *Völsunga Saga* is another 13th century work, though it is believed to be based on far older source material. The actual author of this tale is not known. Among many elements, the saga recounts the wars between the Burgundians, Huns, and the Goths. It is quite an epic tale that even includes dragon slaying. This saga inspired several other such as J. R. R. Tolkien and Richard Wagner. However, the focus here will only be on its first couple of chapters. Once again, we only have a brief mention of Frigg, but it alludes to a good deal more.

The story begins with a man named Sigi who is a son of Odin. On one occasion Sigi and Bredi, the thrall of another man, went hunting together. Bredi ended up with the largest catch of the day. This angered Sigi and so he killed Bredi and buried him in a snowdrift. When Sigi returned he said that Bredi had ridden away into the forest and Sigi did not know what became of him.

His story was doubted, and they suspected Sigi of deception. A search party was sent out, and Bredi's body was recovered. This in turn revealed that Sigi had killed Bredi. He was then branded an outlaw who could no longer remain in Odin's home.

Odin guided Sigi, and some troops, to a warship. Sigi and the troops took to raiding, and eventually they were able to take control of a kingdom. Sigi and his wife went on to have a son they named Rerir. Then came the day that Sigi's brother-in-laws attacked and killed Sigi and his men. Luckily, Rerir was not present at that time. When he learned of what had occurred, he took some time, but eventually gathered enough forces to retake the kingdom. He became an influential king, perhaps even more so than his father.

Rerir took a wife and the two tried for many years to produce a child without any luck. They finally begged the gods for a child, and "It is said that Frigg heard their prayers and told Odin what they asked" (Byock, 1990, p. 36). Odin then sent the Valkyrie Hljod, daughter of the jotunn Hrimnir, with an apple to bestow it on Rerir and his wife. Rerir assumed it was from Frigg and Odin, so he took the apple home to his queen and ate it.

The queen soon found herself pregnant. Unfortunately, the pregnancy continued on with no end in sight. After some time, Rerir fell ill and died. After six years of being with child the queen asked for the child to be cut from her. When they did the boy was nearly grown, and he kissed his mother before she slipped away. This boy was named Volsung, and he became king as his father was. Hrimnir then sent Hljod to be with Volsung. Together Volsung and Hljod had ten sons and a daughter who all grew to achieve great accomplishments.

The saga does go on from there, but Frigg has no other role in the remainder of it. We see Frigg in this story being the goddess who responds first to the situation. At the very least she is the one receptive to the prayers, and it is she that alerts Odin. This is like what we see in *Oddrúnargrátr* with Frigg being a goddess connected in some form with childbirth. Now, the six yearlong pregnancy is probably not one anybody would say is a prayer come true. However, the couple did eventually receive the blessings of a very successful offspring; who himself went on to produce many more accomplished children of his own with Hljod. This example displays that as a devoted mother herself, praying to Frigg in matters of childbirth and childrearing can only be beneficial.

Egil's Saga

Egil's Saga focuses on the family of the poet and farmer Egil Skallagrimsson. The saga spans around 150 years and deals a lot with the family's feud with the kings of Norway. As such, much of the story takes place in Norway, though it spans much of the Viking world of that time. It is thought to be composed in the 13th century as the other sagas outlined here, but it takes place between the years 850-1000 (Smiley et al., 2000). Though the author of this saga is not known for certain, the most common consensus is that it was composed by Snorri Sturluson, said to be a descendent of Egil.

This is a lengthy saga, but the area of interest for this book is Chapter 79. In this chapter Egil's daughter, Thorgerd, has asked Egil to compose a poem in memory of Egil's sons, Bodvar and Gunnar, who have both died. Egil, being particularly distraught after the recent loss of Bodvar, was doubtful of his ability to compose a poem under these circumstances, but he does give it a go. The result is a beautiful poem known as *Sonatorrek*. I have included the first three stanzas below, but it is in the second stanza that we will see an important reference to Frigg.

My tongue is sluggish / for me to move, / my poem's scales / ponderous to raise. / The god's prize / is beyond my grasp, / tough to drag out / from my mind's haunts.

32

Since heavy sobbing / is the cause- / how hard to pour forth / from the mind's root / the prize that Frigg's / progeny found, borne of old / from the world of giants,
unflawed, which Bragi / inspired with life / on the craft / of the watcher-dwarf. / Blood surges / from the giant's wounded neck, / crashes on the death-dwarf's / boathouse door (Smiley et al., 2000, p. 152).

In the second stanza we see the gods referred to collectively as "Frigg's progeny." This is certainly interesting as it seems to convey that all the Æsir are her children. However, it is most certainly a symbolic title for Frigg. Still, while it is common to call Odin the "All-Father" we see little such references to Frigg specifically. This does seem to imply that she was seen as the Germanic "All-Mother" to at least some.

Trójumanna Saga

The *Trójumanna Saga*, thought to be composed sometime in the 13th century, is the Norse version of the events that took place during the Trojan War. This version uses Norse goddesses as glosses for the Hellenic ones. In the seventh chapter of the saga the names of Venus, Hera, and Athena are replaced with Freyja, Sif and Gefjun, respectively. However, in the following chapter Gefjun is replaced with Frigg. I find it interesting that Frigg is directly referenced as being a "god of battle" in this text (Sigurðsson, 1848). It is hard to determine if the author intentionally replaced Frigg for Gefjun, or if it was in error. Regarding Frigg, Näsström (1995) states that: "...here she is obviously misinterpreted as Gefjun" (p. 109). Either way, this example lends some credence to the linking of these two goddesses. I will discuss the connection of Frigg and Gefjun further in Chapter 5.

Personal Take

This chapter probably constituted tales that are much more familiar to the average student of Norse mythology. That being said, I hope that I included a few that you may not have otherwise known. The Edda's are both known to view Frigg as the devoted wife to Odin and the loving mother of Baldr. These are two of the first things I ever learned of Frigg many years ago. The heartbreak that Frigg felt at the loss of Baldr, and then of Odin, is probably more than many can even bear to imagine. Still, she somehow finds the inner strength to continue after the fact.

It is in these roles that her function as a mother, in all its manifestations, is brought to light. This connection to motherhood is brought to even further fruition in the sagas when the gods are lovingly referred to as her progeny. The role of motherhood is one that I feel is glossed over so easily in our society. Frigg is the foundation of the Norse gods so to speak, and we would do well not to forget that. Without a solid foundation, whole structures would crumble. Frigg serves as my spiritual mother, and without her today I do not know where I would be. The All-Mother seeks to lend a hand when we cannot get up but give us that strength to stand on our own.

Chapter 3

Roles and Symbols of Frigg

This chapter will be an examination into the various roles and symbols of Frigg. While I feel that the gods are far more than the singular roles that we commonly assign to them, I still feel their impact in certain areas. This is true of Frigg. It is easy to say Frigg is the 'Hearth Goddess' or the 'Goddess of Marriage,' but there are many other areas where I feel her resonate. I hope to highlight many of the traits here, but Frigg is much more than this chapter can include. She is chief counsel in many aspects of my life, and some have little to do with the following aspects. So, seek her out and see the unique roles that she may show to you.

Love

I chose to begin with the role of love because Frigg is connected to it by her very name. In the simplest terms we can call Frigg a goddess of love. I think that many would point out that the love Frigg represents is that of the love a wife has for her husband, the love a mother has for her child, or the love someone has for a dear friend. These same voices would refer to Freyja as governing over the more carnal side of love. However, while these can be distinct forms of love, I find it much too restrictive. The love a wife has for her husband should be one of many forms. Spiritual, emotional, but I would imagine it to be carnal as well. At least from time to time. I see no reason both Frigg and Freyja cannot hold sway over love in all its forms.

So, turn to Frigg in all these matters. Whatever is stirring in your heart I feel that she can lend her assistance. Is there a fresh new love in your life that you are not sure how to handle? Pray to Frigg for guidance. Has your long marriage hit a bump, or perhaps has grown slightly stagnant? Make an offering to Frigg and ask for ideas on how to turn up the heat. Struggling with an unruly teenager that you cannot figure out? Sit in meditation with Frigg to search for tips. No, I have no children, but I was that unruly teenager. Though my mother handled me quite well I am sure she would have appreciated any advice. Frigg and her role as a goddess of love has much to offer us.

Personally, there was a period of my life, not so long ago, that I gave up on love having resigned myself to a life of solitude. I have always been socially withdrawn and going out to meet guys just did not suit me. Then, out of nowhere, I did meet someone via social media, and we quickly fell in love. We were married a year from the day that we first started dating. It has not been all roses and rainbows, but it is a happy marriage and I thank Frigg for that every day. She is the one that I credit with showing me just how to love again.

Marriage

Though much of this topic was covered under love, I felt it deserving of its own entry. Marriage is a complicated beast. Growing over the years and learning who we are and what our purpose in life is can be quite the journey. Throw in another person and learning to navigate who that person is can be an entirely different matter. I grew up knowing I was gay from nearly as far back as I have memories. I may not have always understood what that meant, but I figured it out at an early age. I never felt I would have the pleasure of sharing my love with another man, but did I ever dream about it.

Married life took a lot of getting used to. I had been single for so long and lived by myself for so many years. It had just been me and the gods (and my dogs) for such a long time. I did not know if I could make the adjustment. We suffered through many arguments in those first few months of dating as we were both so new to all of this. I think many would have given up, but we both knew it was love. I just needed to find some way to navigate things. Frigg showed up and taught me to do just that.

I feel that it was a direct result of Frigg's guiding hand that allowed me to step back and take stock of the situation before ending things too abruptly. In the past I would have jumped ship at the first sign of rough waters. I knew that I cared too much to give up, but I was not sure what steps to take next. I started to hear myself before I would react to a fight about ready to erupt. It was as if a voice would say, "Hey, think before you speak!" I would heed this advice and take careful consideration of what came out of my mouth. This was not one-sided by any means. I feel that in my process of thoughtful speech that my husband learned the same techniques. I would later confirm that the voice I heard was Frigg. It was through Frigg's tutelage that made that first passionate year one of great learning and success. Frigg is a goddess of marital peace after all, and she taught me how to obtain that in my own home. Remember to call out to her when you need solace, but never forget to thank her for the blessings in marriage that you already do have.

All-Mother

I feel it has been well established that Frigg is the All-Mother. As the ever-loving, fighter of a mother in the story of Baldr that I covered, she is the relentless aid. Unfortunately, in the case of Baldr, things did not turn out well. Perhaps that is why she has become such a mother figure to so many others; gods and humans alike. It is the inspiration of Frigg in my life that leads me to be a better custodian to the people, and animals, I surround myself with.

I have no human children to relate to this role, and even if I did, I will never be a mother. So, to say I can understand this aspect of Frigg would be disingenuous. However, one way that I can connect with this role is as a son who has a mother that is quite reminiscent of Frigg. My mother has always been someone

I could turn to when I am in need. She has been a constant rock in my life that I will forever be grateful for. At the same time, she has allowed me to stand up on my own when she knew that I could. I have relied on my mother over the years, but because of the gifts she has imparted I can stand on my own and be proud. I see these exact qualities in Frigg.

Another aspect of my life that I can very loosely attach the moniker of 'mother' is my role as a caretaker to my dogs. I know it sounds cliché to many, but they are my children. I would do anything in my power to see their tails wag. I feel that being a dog dad is a constant duty. I have had at least two dogs at a time in my care for many years now. I feel it is a personal obligation to care for dogs in need. I need to be that rock for them. I always take in rescue dogs, and they are with me for the remainder of their, hopefully, long lives. I mourn their loss and can never replace them, but my custodial obligations will continue. This is all due to the counsel of my physical real-world mother, and my spiritual mother; Frigg.

Queen

I initially had two sections here, one for "Queen" and one for "Sovereignty." The more I thought about it the more I saw the two linked and so here we are. As the wife of Odin, Frigg is the designated Queen of the Æsir and Asynjur. When Odin went away on his journey in the *Ynglinga Saga*, both Vili and Ve took over as the de facto kings. However, Frigg remained in her position. In fact, for them to truly rule they had to 'take' Frigg as well. It appears their right to rule was dependent on Frigg's approval. She provided this, but as soon as Odin returned, he quickly regained his rule. Frigg's position never faltered.

Turn to Frigg in matters of sovereignty. This, depending on the situation, can be literal or figurative. Maybe you are in a position of authority at work, and you find yourself losing your voice. Learn from Frigg the ability to command respect. Just keep in mind, Frigg always is a generous leader and never a tyrant. Do not let that power go to your head, or you may risk losing that position. Perhaps you are dealing with a situation establishing boundaries with a problematic person in your life. Learn to hold your ground here as well. Seek out the wisdom of Frigg. Know when to let the love flow, and when to shut down the detractors to be a just queen.

Peace-Keeper

One area of which Frigg holds sway that is often overlooked is that of a goddess of peace. In *Lokasenna* specifically, we are witness to her attempts to subdue Loki by peaceful means. Rather than fight, Frigg hopes that Loki will cease his taunts and that everyone will get along. This is quite in line with her role as both a queen and a mother. A queen likely has an interest in keeping the peace between rivals within her kingdom. Likewise, a mother has a personal stake in keeping the peace between squabbling siblings. Frigg concerns herself with this in a noble fashion. It is important for the betterment of everyone that things can be worked out without any drastic infighting. Even in the story about the naming of the Lombards where Frigg intervenes on their behalf before a great battle, we see this. Odin said that he would grant victory to the first one that he sees upon sunrise, and she successfully maneuvers events on the Lombards behalf. A story about how a war saw less bloodshed because of her direct intervention.

Hearth & Home

As a goddess of love, marriage, motherhood, and sovereignty I feel that the role as a 'Hearth and Home Goddess' simply falls into place. The hearth, as a physical designation, is not such a common object in our homes anymore. However, a while back, the hearth was the center of the home. It was truly the epicenter of everything that went down. Food was cooked there, and the family would keep warm at its side. Its importance cannot be overstated. Likewise, the importance of the hearth goddess cannot be over emphasized. Today, our stoves and furnaces can provide this center of our homes as they dispense similar services. Additionally, if you have a spot for your main altar this can function as your home's spiritual center.

As the goddess of the home Frigg is a natural attendant to the keys of said household. It was a frequent practice for the woman to hold the keys on a belt as she oversaw all duties relating to the realm of domestic activities. Keys were representative of a woman's power in that arena. Keys come in many forms today. From the shiny metal devices that we use to unlock our house, to the passwords we keep on our computer, and everything in between, keys are vitally important. Keys serve to represent what is sacred, and what is hidden. They are the 'key' to accessing those things we wish to keep out of prying hands and eyes. So, hold tightly to all your keys whether they are physical, or metaphorical in nature. Guard what is deemed sacred to you, and may Frigg offer you security.

On a personal note, when I first met my husband, I was in a situation where I found myself unable to work due to a disability. As he was working, I found myself falling into the role of the homemaker. This is not a role in life I had ever imagined, and it was a difficult adjustment. At first, I felt it was required of me to do this work so that I could pull my own weight in the relationship. I found no joy when I felt it was something that I had to do to be on equal footing. Then things began to change. It felt good having a house that felt like a home. When I was able, I enjoyed cooking dinner and having it ready for him when he would arrive home. It was a subtle change that I still cannot explain, but my outlook was different. It is hard work running a household, however, I found that it was equally rewarding as well. I must admit, I am by no means the perfect person at tending to a home. I have days when my pain is so extreme that I get nothing accomplished. Still, it is important work that I now enjoy doing whenever I can. This work is done with a lot of heart and purpose in mind, and it is done in Frigg's name.

Prophecy

One trait of Frigg that is repeated time and again is that she knows, but does not speak, the fates. So why her refusal to reveal what she sees? Perhaps it was the horrific failure to alter the outcome of Baldr's life? This could cause great emotional scarring. So maybe Frigg does have the ability to see all, but she refuses to reveal what she knows because the outcome will not change. Perhaps Frigg does not speak of future events because it brings the event closer to fruition? For instance, speaking of the future may naturally seal its inevitability.

The case of Loki is a curious one, however. While Frigg can foresee future events, and takes steps to alter their outcome, she is unable to see what Loki is truly up to. If she were, then she would not have divulged the secret about the mistletoe. This could be due to some unknown power of Loki to thoroughly shield his disguise and innocence. I feel that there must be more to the story. Maybe Frigg has a blind spot when it comes to jotnar and she is unable to foresee their actions?

One theory is that perhaps what Frigg knows is our ørlǫg. This essentially means "original law," and would be fate that has already come to pass. If this is what Frigg can see, then it would make sense that she is unable to foresee what is truly to become of Baldr. Knowledge of ørlǫg is a form of knowing the fates so this may be a correct assumption. As Loki is hurling insults in *Lokasenna*, predominantly about peoples past actions, then it would make sense that he is warned about Frigg knowing about everyone's past herself.

An additional idea is that maybe she is just unable to see the precise future of those she is closest to; namely that of Baldr and Odin. In the case of Odin, we see that in *Vafþrúðnismál*

Frigg cautions him against going to the home of Vafþruðnir to challenge him. She seems hesitant to offer him her approval for this but stops short of saying something bad *will* happen. Maybe this is why she offers caution instead of pleading that Odin does not go. If she is unable to see, or cannot see what will really transpire clearly, then she cannot know for certain whether something good or bad will eventually occur. Frigg simply offers her opinion, and then later tells him to be safe. This could also be because Vafþruðnir is a jotunn, just as Loki is a jotunn. This could imply that her blind spot is not for Odin and Baldr, but for the jotnar themselves as stated above.

At any rate, we know that Frigg is a goddess that knows the fates but does not speak of them. One would think that she would be a powerful ally in divination techniques, but that does not seem to be the case. For that I suggest you become an ally to Vör who will be discussed in Chapter 5. That being said, it cannot hurt to have a powerful friend in Frigg that can still see the fates. While she may not reveal what is to happen, we can rest assured that she will do everything in her power to try and keep us safe from harm.

Healer

While not a well-known guise, the role of healer is yet another to add to this growing list. In the *Second Merseburg Incantation* we see that Frigg, along with Volla (Fulla), work their charms to assist in the healing of a horse. In addition to Frigg and Fulla, we will also learn that their close associate in the healing arts is Eir. Together these three are a powerful healing combination. I have seen fit to call on Frigg numerous times when healing assistance was needed. I can say from personal experience that I have felt her healing energy at work.

Offering prayers, and actual physical offerings, are an effective way to get the ball rolling. I never ask a favor of the gods if I do not have a working reciprocal relationship with them. Imagine having never spoken with a person and they just come to you asking for favors. I cannot see that going over well, and this is no different with the divine. That is not to say that emergencies do not come up. We may be faced with a matter of great urgency and in our hour of need we ask Frigg for her help. I would just see to it that as soon as possible an offering was made in return; regardless of the outcome. Sometimes the gods help in ways that are not immediately apparent.

I have also found that her healing works are not confined to people. I had a recent medical emergency with one of my dogs due to an attack from another dog. I made several prayers and offerings to see that my fur-baby pulled through okay. I am happy to report that, minus a couple of minor scars, she did pull through relatively unharmed. This is no surprise to me as the *Second Merseburg Incantation* involved the healing of an animal itself. Pets are a part of our families and Frigg recognizes that when lending her assistance.

Holistic health and the healing arts were both things that I have enjoyed for some time. I began searching for ways to further pursue these interests in part because of Frigg. It was on that path that I discovered the ability to make soap from scratch. Not just any soap, I make good soap. A hard bar of soap that lasts long, suds well, and does not dry out the skin. It took some time to develop recipes that worked like they did, but I had fun experimenting. I eventually expanded my repertoire to include herbal balms and lotions. This has not only become a hobby, but I passion of mine. One that I may not have discovered without welcoming Frigg into my life.

Spinning and Weaving

As a goddess of the hearth and home it should come as no surprise that various domestic arts and crafts fall under the purview of Frigg. Although in our disposable society it is hard to see their importance, spinning and weaving once formed an important part of the lives of women in times gone by. The women were responsible for creating all the clothes on the backs of family members and that cannot be overlooked; especially in northern climates. We do have evidence of Frigg being seen as a spinner in Scandinavia. The term *Friggerock* we saw can mean either "Frigg's Spindle," "Frigg's Spinning Wheel," or some variety thereof as a name for Orion's Belt. Davidson (2001) also notes that spinning in Blekinge Sweden was not permitted on Thursdays; "as that was when Frigg's spinning was done" (p. 104).

As a goddess of spinning and weaving the distaff serves as an important symbol for Frigg. Much like the keys represent her connection to the home itself, the distaff serves as a reminder of the important household duties that fell on the wife. In addition, the spinning wheel and spindle are good representatives for Frigg. These symbols amount to more than just their mundane purposes. It is important as well to see spinning and weaving as a metaphor. This is the case with weaving peaceful environments, and the spinning of fate. Frigg is a masterclass at keeping her cool in stressful situations, and always looking for a peaceful outcome. Likewise, as a goddess of ørlǫg she is represented by spinning the threads of fate as they are each then placed down throughout our lives.

Fertility

There are numerous reasons to link Frigg to fertility. This is fertility in all its guises. First off, she is a mother, a love goddess, and connected with childbirth. These three reasons alone may fulfill this role. On top of that, she is possibly connected with the gift of sovereignty of the land for her relationships with Vili and Ve. This may even include Odin's right to rule if we are to follow that line of thought. She may also be the daughter of the god Fjörgynn who is, at least in name, connected to the earth goddess Fjörgyn. Some have even put forth the idea that Jörd (Earth) is simply a byname of Frigg (Davidson, 2001). Finally, her name being connected to cornfields in Sweden sums up her connection to this role.

So, as a goddess of children and childbirth one could seek out her aid when assistance is required. She is shown in the lore to have helped in conception on at least one occasion. This connection to fertility carries right over into the fertility of the earth as well. Frigg can be seen as a grain mother, and of the fruitful earth herself. Seek out her aid in gardening related endeavors. This ties up nicely with her role as a goddess of the home as well. The vegetable garden being a natural outdoor extension of the kitchen. I feel that this is an often-overlooked area of Frigg's sphere of influence that she indeed takes a great interest in.

Animals

Many deities are associated with various animals. In the Norse pantheon we have examples such as Odin with wolves and ravens, Freyja with cats, and Thor with goats. While we do not see Frigg specifically associated with any animals, apart from the hawk/falcon, we can still infer some from the information that we do have. As an animist, animals do play a significant role on my path. Below are just a few of the animals that I connect to Frigg in some form or another.

Hawk/Falcon

Frigg is said to possess either a hawk or falcon cloak that enables her to fly through the skies. It is for this reason that I have included them here first. It is the only animal that is directly connected with her in the lore. The hawk is representative of the sky, and Frigg is a sky goddess in many respects. Their keen eyesight of these birds of prey is another link to Frigg who sees and knows all. As successful hunters these birds are required by their nature to be very intelligent. This intelligence is similar to what Frigg displays in her battles with Odin.

Hawk is more of a catchall term for many birds of prey, and they have near global distribution. Falcons also live on every continent apart from Antarctica. As such, I do not feel that one species holds any sway over the others when it comes to connecting to Frigg. Where I am from, the Red-Tailed Hawk is very common and is an apex predator. This has been the species that I have come to associate most closely with Frigg. However, the Osprey has been spreading its territory to include my area of the country as well. The Osprey is intricately linked with water and wetlands, so I feel that they have a special connection to Frigg.

Heron/Crane

I felt that both herons and cranes deserved an honorable mention here. The heron is another bird with a near global reach. Though only linked to Cranes by a general appearance, I have included them as well. However, I will specifically deal with herons, and more precisely the Great Blue Heron. The Great Blue Heron is a magnificent bird. They also exhibit intelligence and are fierce hunters; though their dominion is primarily as a hunter in shallow waters. They can sit for hours stalking their prey. Their generous size keeps most predators at bay. I have seen them called the *Queen of the Marsh* on numerous occasions, and what an apt title for a bird connected to Frigg.

Geese

Geese, ducks, swans, and the like, are very representative of Frigg. These make sense not only because of their superb mothering qualities, but many species even mate for life. This goes without mentioning their innate connection to all things aquatic. I cannot help but think of the endearing Mother Goose nursery rhymes that my mother would read to me as a child. Some of these stories have been told to children for hundreds of years. Grimm postulated the theory that Mother Goose was related to Berchta, a figure from German myth, who has also been linked to Frigg on occasion. In any case, the connection between geese and Frigg is one that I feel can be readily felt.

Sheep/Ram

The association with Frigg and rams is a relatively recent one. It is believed to have been developed by Richard Wagner for his four-part operatic epic The Ring of the Nibelung, or *Der Ring des Nibelungen*. Still, I think they may be one of the most appropriate animals to connect to Frigg. Her strong relationship with spinning makes this an obvious choice, but as a domesticated animal we find another link. As a goddess of all things domestic Frigg has a natural proclivity to work with sheep. While she may have a hawk cloak enabling her to soar through the air, I can just as easily imagine her flying through the skies in a chariot led by rams. Think what you will of Wagner and his interpretations, but I think he was spot on with this idea.

Dog

The last animal I have chosen to include is the dog. Again, this is personal interpretation when it comes to this connection. Perhaps I am biased in my envisioning Frigg with a connection to dogs given my personal link to them, but it feels so natural. I cannot think of a better animal to associate with all things domestic. Not only are dogs domesticated animals, but one of their chief duties to this day is guarding the home. While we may possess keys to lock people out, or furry friends often stay behind to watch the gates as it were. What better companion is there than a dog? (I see you cat people). Truth be told, I love cats as well, but I think we all see them as under the jurisdiction of Freyja. Also, while they are technically domesticated, I do not feel that cats would agree with that terminology.

Dogs are a constant rock in my life, and my relationship with Frigg is amplified by the love I share with my canine companions. I see the two as going hand in hand. My dogs keep me up and busy even when I do not feel that I can get up to tend to them. I must find a way no matter where my pain levels are at. So, in that essence, they keep me up working around the home. If I must get up and let them outside then I may as well empty the dishwasher while I am up, right? Taking care of dogs is a labor of love for me that goes right along with running a household.

Fensalir

We will finally discuss Fensalir here. I previously mentioned that this translates to something along the lines of "Marsh Halls" though I have seen others as well. One such name is by Turville-Petre (1964) which is the very similar "Water Halls" (p. 189). As you can see, there is little distinction between the two with both offering aquatic imagery. This is more than likely the source of Frigg's relationship with water, and this makes sense. As the All-Mother and Queen, I am sure she could have chosen any location to live, but she chose near the water. I have always personally envisioned her hall near a marsh. It is just how it has come to me. However, it could just as likely be near a lake or the sea.

Wherever you see it, water holds a great deal of symbolism. Water is mysterious and powerful. In some cultures, the land of the dead is on the other side of a body of water. Water is often used in scrying methods as well. I can picture Frigg sitting on a porch that overlooks the wetland and peering in to see some hidden truth. While I personally find great joy visiting my local wetlands, I can imagine that in times of sorrow it fosters that emotion as well. We know that Frigg went to Fensalir to weep after Baldr's death. I can also imagine a warm fire going in her great hall as she builds great memories with her handmaidens.

These local wetlands that I alluded to are very special to me. There are two locations that I live nearby. I connect with many deities there, but here I will discuss Frigg. It is hauntingly beautiful for starters. Seeing a Great Blue Heron as she sits silently by awaiting her next meal. Her blue-grey plumage is nearly the same color I see Frigg wearing. I am sure that aids in my connection between the two. While there are no structures at either location, if I look hard enough, I can see her great hall out in the middle surrounded by great trees of the marshland. A series of connected plank walkways link her hall to the shore. Inside, great rites are held, and lavish feasts occur. It is a remarkable sight.

Personal Take

This chapter was difficult as I had to do a few things. The first was to relegate common roles to Frigg. This is not something I am prone to do. So often I say that the gods are far more than simple functions, yet here is a chapter dedicated to just that. Second, I had to narrow the many varied parts she does play in my life to just enough that would fill a chapter. Lastly, I had to reduce these expansive roles down to a couple paragraphs each. For some topics this is much easier said than done.

For instance, it was my dedication to my role as a homemaker several years ago that I realized what an important, and often overlooked, function that is. I recall when I was younger, and had vast dreams on a grand scale, asking my mother what she wanted to be growing up. She responded that she wanted to be a wife and a mother. I could not imagine that. I asked again what it was that she wanted to do with her life. She reiterated that she was doing what she had always wanted to do. It would be a quarter of a century before I found the importance in doing what I had watched her do effortlessly for so many years and that I took for granted.

I hope that I imparted some insight into these roles and symbols of Frigg. I did try to pull as much from the sources as possible when compiling it. However, much of this chapter was informed by personal gnosis. It is my hope that it can still help you in some manner on your path. These aspects, objects, and animals really helped me to grow my practice into what it is today. As I said, Frigg is far more than what I was able to present here. This was just an introduction to a few of the varied guises that Frigg possesses.

Chapter 4

Deities Associated with Frigg

Frigg serves as the matriarch of the Æsir family of gods and goddesses. As such, she is related to many popular figures in various ways. In this chapter I will examine these relationships. You can tell a lot about someone from the company that they keep. Further examination of these relationships can only serve to increase our understanding of Frigg. I will begin by highlighting Frigg's parental relationships, or what little information is known about them. Next, I will look to her husband and children to help identify some of her more well-known attributes; that of being a wife and mother. Finally, I decided to end this chapter by examining a goddess to whom she is most frequently linked. This is the goddess Freyja. Though the two share some functional overlap, I will seek to address whether they are the same or different deities. Hopefully by the culmination of this chapter you will gain a better understanding of Frigg through these relationships.

Family of Frigg

As already referenced, Frigg is well known for the role she plays as the matriarch of her family, and the Æsir as a whole. Indeed, in *Egil's Saga* we saw that the gods are collectively seen as the children of Frigg. Some of the members of this family are well known and established as relatives. However, there does remain some inconclusiveness as to a few other facts such as her parents and some of her offspring, for instance.

Parents

We know very little concrete information regarding Frigg's parentage. In the *Prose Edda* we discovered that in most translations Frigg is seen as the daughter of Fjörgynn such as in *Gylfaginning* 9. In *Skáldskaparmál* the kenning for Frigg as "the daughter of Fjörgynn" was given (Sturluson & Brodeur, 1916, p. 129). We saw this repeated in the *Poetic Edda* in *Lokasenna* where Loki is insulting Frigg. The name "Fjörgynn" is typically seen as the masculine form of "Fjörgyn," another name given as Thor's mother that also means "Earth." If Fjörgyn and Fjörgynn are connected, either as a couple or the same deity under different names, then there is a chance that Frigg and Thor are siblings in addition to Frigg being Thor's stepmother. Simek (2007) notes that attempts have been made to connect Fjörgynn to the Lithuanian Perkunas, a thunder god. However, he continues to say that this may be "reading too much into the 12th and 13th century recordings of the name" (p. 86).

Some translations do not seem to differentiate between the masculine and feminine forms at all making it hard to determine the authors opinion on the matter. Both Byock (2005) and Crawford (2015), in the Prose Edda and Poetic Edda respectively, record the name of Frigg's parent in the form of "Fjörgyn." I am not knowledgeable enough in Old Norse to recognize the differences in the masculine and feminine forms other than noting the extra "n" on the masculine form. To make matters even more confusing some authors replace "daughter" with "wife" (Bellows, 1936, p. 160) or simply "girl" (Crawford, 2015, p. 106). In the original text the term is *mær* which can be translated variously as "maid, girl, virgin or daughter." As you can imagine, this makes it difficult to determine the actual relationship that Frigg has with this figure.

Spouse

If the parents of Frigg are not confidently known, we have witnessed ample resources that indicate one thing, and that is the spouse of Frigg. In early southern Germanic, and Scandinavian sources alike, we are told that Frigg is the wife of

Odin. The one-eyed chief god of the Æsir is notorious in Norse mythology. Odin is known under various spellings of his name such as Óðinn in Old Norse, Woden in Old English, Wodan in Old High German, and Godan among the Lombards. The name is often Anglicized as Odin, and for the sake of simplicity this is the name I have chosen to use for him here. The name Odin is the source of our modern English Wednesday. This comes from the Old English Wōdnesdæg meaning "day of Woden." This is in part due to his designation as the Germanic counterpart to the Roman Mercury.

He also lends his name to various locations throughout the Germanic lands particularly in Denmark and England. For instance, in England there is Wenslow, Wedynsfeld, Wodnesfeld, and Wansdyke all believed to have been named for him (Simek, 2007). This serves as an attestation to the importance that his cult once held. Odin's numerous roles help lend to his widely held worship. These include a god of healing, prophecy, poetry, wisdom, and war, among other designations. He earned his status as a one-eyed god by sacrificing one of his eyes for a single drink from the Well of Mimir, known for its ability to impart vast amounts of wisdom. This action of self-sacrifice is not the only one that Odin partakes in. He also stabs himself with his spear, Gungnir, and hanged himself from Yggdrasil in order to obtain the knowledge of the runes.

He is given many bynames such as Grim, Harbard, Gaut, and Ygg, just to name a few. He is also called, and considered to be, the All-Father. Indeed, he serves as the Royal ancestor of most of the historic kingdoms of Anglo-Saxon England. I will discuss some of his godly children momentarily but suffice it to say he is thought to have fathered many of them with various jotnar. Still, Frigg has remained his wife through it all. As the wife of Odin, Frigg is often considered the queen of the Æsir. Odin is referred to as *Friggs Faðmbyggvi*, meaning 'dweller in Frigg's embrace,' in the *Haraldskvæði* (Grundy, 2002, p. 62).

This is one of the oldest of skaldic poems that remain today. Interestingly, the skald *Hallfreðr Vandræðaskáld* uses the kenning *Frumverr Friggjar*, meaning 'Frigg's original, or first husband,' in reference to Odin (Näsström, 1995, p. 107).

As I have shown, the myths often indicate a bit of rivalry between Odin and Frigg. On at least two occasions they each pick a given side in a dispute and attempt various maneuvers to one-up the other. It could be argued that in both instances it is Frigg that comes out on top in these situations. These opposing positions do not seem to cause any rifts in their marriage. The myths also present, at least once, that Odin seeks out the wise counsel of Frigg. This shows a level of trust that Odin places in his wife's charge.

In addition to Frigg's marriage to Odin I found an odd piece of information in my research. Näsström (1995) writes that according to Hyltén-Cavallius, in his work *Wärend och Wirdarne*, it was common in Sweden to refer to Thursday as *signa Thore-Gud ok Frigge*, meaning "Hallow the god Þórr and Frigge" (p. 106). The implication of this being that: "Frigg was, according to popular belief, the wife of Þórr and accompanied him on his travels – a conception also found in other parts of Sweden and Denmark" (p. 106). This is the only place I have ever found such a reference, so I do not know if this holds any weight. However, I thought it was important to include it here for reference. I personally understand this to imply that marriage itself was considered sacred to Thor and Frigg. In particular, Thursday evening would make a good deal of sense, if this were true, as it would fall between Thursday and Friday; days sacred to Thor and Frigg, respectively. In my personal work I only see Frigg as the wife of Odin.

Child

Although Odin is known to have fathered numerous children, Frigg is identified specifically as the mother of just one of them. This would be the shining god Baldr. The relationship between Frigg and Baldr is quite endearing. Frigg and Baldr are particularly renowned for the story found in *Gylfaginning* 49. The loss of Baldr would be one of the great sorrows of her life. This story shows both the heartache, and strength, of Frigg. Above any other story, I feel this is the tale that solidifies her role as a goddess of motherhood.

In the poem *Lokasenna*, it is Baldr whom Frigg claims would be her savior when Loki taunts Frigg. She appears to defer to the idea of Baldr's protection even though her husband Odin is present there. I am not sure if this says more for Frigg and her relationship with Baldr, or that of Frigg and Odin. Baldr seems to have been the most loved by all the gods. With the obvious exclusion of Loki. Sturluson reports of Baldr that: "He is so beautiful and so bright that light shines from him" (Sturluson & Byock, 2005, p. 33). He also reports that Baldr is the wisest of the gods. His hall is called Breiðablik, meaning "the far-shining one" in Old Norse (Simek, 2007). Of this hall, Sturluson states: "It is in heaven, and no impurity may be there" (Sturluson and Byock, 2005, p. 33).

Frigg and Baldr may appear together in the early continental *Second Merseburg Incantation*, though as discussed earlier, the identities of the various figures is not known with certainty. In addition, a figure named Bældæg appears in the royal genealogies of England. This could be thought of as the Old English equivalent to Baldr, but this is uncertain.

Stepchildren

Aside from Baldr, there are numerous gods who could be considered the stepsons of Frigg. Chief among these is the god, Thor. Thor is the son of Odin and Jörd, meaning "Earth." I should mention here that there is a school of thought that believes Jörd to be another name for Frigg. Davidson (2001) expresses this viewpoint when she says, "...she [Frigg] bore the name Jörd (Earth)" (p. 146). The name Thor means "thunder" and he is among the most honored of the Norse gods in both the past and present. Thor lends his name to the modern English Thursday. Many places throughout the Germanic lands are named for him. In Iceland alone around 20 such places are to be found (Turville-Petre, 1964). As previously alluded to, Frigg's mysterious parentage may mean that Thor is in fact a sibling to her. In addition, we have the previous theory that the two were popularly thought to be married in parts of Sweden and Denmark.

Two other gods are mentioned as sons of Odin. There is Vidar and Vali. Odin fathered Vidar with the jotunn Grid. Simek (2007) notes that Vidar is considered the strongest of the gods after Thor. Vali, who Odin fathered with the jotunn Rind, was born for the sole purpose of being Baldr's avenger and killing Hodr. Both Vidar and Vali are among the younger generation of gods that will survive Ragnarok.

Various other gods are mentioned in different contexts as sons of Odin, but it is unclear if these are just kennings, or if they are actually his sons. Among these are; Bragi, Tyr, and Heimdall. Bragi is the god of poetry who is married to Idunn. Tyr is the one-handed god of battle. Elsewhere his father is given as the jotunn Hymir. Although Tyr features little in Norse myths his name is cognate with other Indo-European sky gods. This may mean that his cult was once highly regarded but diminished by the time the myths were recorded. Heimdall is said in *Völuspá* 1 to be the father of humankind (Crawford, 2015). He plays the role of the watchman of the gods where he stands guard at the Bifrost bridge. Heimdall is said to be the son of nine mothers who some assume to be the nine daughters of Aegir (Simek, 2007).

In addition to these last three is Hermod and Hodr. Hermod is the one who rides on Odin's horse Sleipnir to Hel to try and retrieve Baldr. Hermod brings back Odin's ring, Draupnir, from

Baldr, and Nanna gives Hermod a linen for Frigg and a gold ring for Fulla. Simek points out that Hermod is only given as a god by Sturluson, and that when he appears elsewhere, he is not viewed as such. Hodr is the blind god who accidentally kills Baldr by shooting him with mistletoe guided by Loki. His name means "warrior, fighter" in Old Norse (Simek, 2007). In the Edda's, Hodr plays the part of a supporting character. However, in Saxo's work he is named Hotherus and he plays a much more prominent role. In this version he is a mortal hero that battles Baldr and wins the hand of Nanna. Hodr presents an interesting case. I have seen him listed many times as the twin brother of Baldr. Unfortunately, I have never read this directly in the sources. The two do pose an interesting list of differences. Baldr is the bright god, while Hodr is blind living his life in the darkness. While Hodr's name means "warrior" Baldr seems like a much more passive god. If Hodr is indeed the twin brother of Baldr that would make him another son of both Odin and Frigg.

Frigg and Freyja

Many have written a great deal about Frigg and Freyja. I thought that it was important to at least touch on the subject here. These two have been compared by scholars for quite some time. The common theories seem to fall into several categories. Some feel that they are the same goddess under different names, some feel that they are separate goddesses, others speculate that they are separate goddesses who share a common origin, and finally others that they were separate goddesses that have merged over time.

One of the things that lead people to equate these two goddesses is the certain traits they seem to share. For one, both Frigg and Freyja are said to possess a falcon cloak. Second, they are both involved in stories where they had sex in exchange for jewelry or gold. In *Sörla þáttur*, which is found in the *Flateyjarbok* manuscript, Freyja is said to sleep with four dwarves in exchange for a necklace (Kershaw, 1921). Interestingly, in this same tale it is said that Freyja is Odin's lover. In *Gesta Danorum* it is said that Frigg sleeps with a servant in exchange for the gold from a statue of Odin (Elton, 1905). Finally, and perhaps most persuasively, the names of their husbands have caused many to conflate the two. Frigg is married to Odin and Freyja is said to be married to Óðr. Odin is technically spelled Óðin so they may indeed be the same god. Óðin is the adjectival form of Óðr leading some to feel that Óðr is simply the older form of the name (Grundy, 2002, p. 56). The comparisons between Ódin and Óðr also exist in the myths as both are known for their extended absences away from home.

The fact that Freyja is absent in the record of the southern Germanic world has also aided the speculation that the two were once the same goddess who had split by the time the later Norse myths were recorded. However, this could just as easily prove that they were separate goddesses with Freyja originating in Scandinavia and Frigg from the southern Germanic lands. Although they both appear in a couple lists of goddesses, the two only appear in the same story on two occasions; *Lokasenna* and *Oddrunargratr*. However, there are two other instances where the two may both be alluded to. First, in *Grímnismál* Freyja is mentioned and Frigg is not, but Sága does appear who, as will be covered later, may be a byname for Frigg. The second occurrence is in *Völuspá* where Frigg is mentioned and Freyja is not, however there is a mention of "Óðr's maid" which may be a reference to Freyja (Grundy, 2002, p. 62).

These two goddesses also display significant differences. Frigg is always associated with the Æsir and Freyja with the Vanir. Frigg is very much a mother figure and (mostly) devoted wife. Freyja appears to be much more sexually active in the myths. Freyja is closely linked to magic and is said to have taught the Æsir seiðr. Frigg is known to be a great seeress who knows all but does not speak of the fates. This role as a seeress could be seen as a trait more fitting to Freyja, but it is said several times that it is Frigg that knows everyone's fate.

Despite these differences, many scholars believe the two to be aspects of one another. Hilda Ellis Davidson (1993) writes that; "It seems as if these two figures with similar names may indeed be two aspects of the same deity" (p. 108). In addition, she says: "It is possible that while in the figure of Frigg we see the great goddess ruling in the heavens, looking down with Wodan upon earth or sharing Odin's high seat, in Freyja we see rather the goddess as queen of the underworld, at home in the land of the dead" (p. 109). Britt-Mari Näsström (1995) discusses a somewhat similar view when she states; "...the two goddesses have the same origin, comprising two aspects of the Great Goddess, which eventually became various myths about the mourning mother, Frigg, and the voluptuous love goddess Freyja" (p. 99).

Ingunn Asdisardottir raised some interesting points in her work; *Frigg and Freyja: One Great Goddess or Two?* Here she notes all their similarities but highlights their differences and states; "She [Frigg] is, of course, better suited to the Christian ideology that prevailed in Sturlusons time. Freyja on the other hand seems independent and free and her and her realm of power is in definite areas of life; she is goddess of fertility, love, magic and seiðr, even death" (Asdisardottir, 2005, p. 423). However, she also states that; "in her original Indo-Germanic form Frigg was probably a lively fertility deity; something like the Eddic image of Freyja" (p. 420). She seems to conclude that they were two distinct goddesses that were merging by the time the myths were being recorded.

While there are many similarities, I do feel that Frigg and Freyja are each unique goddesses who just happen to have some of their functions overlap. They may have originally been one Great Goddess, or they may indeed have been merging at the time the Edda's were recorded. However, I do feel that the evidence of the Edda's shows the two to be unique deities at the time they were recorded. I also feel that, in an attempt to reverse the common consensus that the two are the same, they have each unfortunately been reduced to simplistic archetypes. I feel that they are distinct, but that does not mean that they cannot oversee similar functions. They are both goddesses that could be called goddesses of love. They are both strong goddesses who are queens of their respective groups. Personally, I feel that blending them into one, as well as placing them into their own specific boxes, is a disservice to them both. Even if there were a way to factually determine that these ancient cultures did view them as the same goddess; I feel that they each have enough people that honor them individually today to confidently say they are separate goddesses.

Personal Take

The family of Frigg, even with the little information that we have, is particularly important to her character. It is unfortunate that we do not have a greater grasp on just who her parents are. We are fortunate to see the dynamic between Frigg and Baldr. As highlighted throughout, she is the mother figure in the Norse myths, so family is extremely critical to her. I feel she takes her role as a mother quite seriously, as one may expect. Even her role as a stepmother seems to be one that she may relish as well.

Her marriage is also a defining factor in her personal traits. While Odin may 'wander' Frigg stays firmly at his side (of course, with a couple of exceptions). It is hard to know if there is an agreement between the two, but I suspect he has her blessing for his extramarital relationships. If Frigg were unhappy in the marriage, I do not think she would stick around. Whatever the case may be, the relationship seems to work for them.

The relationship with Freyja is perhaps the most complicated. Were the originally one goddess, or were they merging at the time the myths were recorded? Without some great discovery on the horizon, we may never know those answers. I think you will find few modern worshipers of either Frigg or Freyja who would say they are the same in our modern world. I find it is better to err on the side of caution in these matters. If they are indeed one "Great Goddess," then I do not think they would care one way or another if they are called Frigg or Freyja. On the other hand, if they are two distinct goddesses, then they just may not appreciate being called by another goddess's name. I have honored both in my practice and the individual offerings to each one has been well received. That, for me, is proof enough.

Chapter 5

The Handmaidens of Frigg

This chapter will focus on Frigg's royal court; popularly known as her handmaidens. In *Gylfaginning* 20 of the *Prose Edda* Sturluson writes; "Not less holy are the Asynjur, the goddesses, and they are of no less authority" (Sturluson & Brodeur, 1916, p. 33). Despite this, many goddesses are only given a sentence regarding their function in the *Prose Edda*. Several of these Asynjur seem to assist Frigg in her activities. In *Gylfaginning* 35 of the *Prose Edda*, there is a list of 16 Asynjur. Frigg is listed as the highest among them. This list also includes Freyja who is referred to as the highest along with Frigg. Sol and Bil are listed last rather passively. Sol is the sun and Bil follows the god Mani, who is the moon, on his journey across the sky. It is the remaining 12 Asynjur that are often referred to as the handmaidens of Frigg. Other terms that may be utilized are ladies-in-waiting or the royal court of Frigg. You will find that I use all three of these terms to refer to them.

Do not let the term handmaiden stop you from honoring them. These are powerful goddesses worthy of veneration. Many Germanic Polytheists have different opinions on them. Some people see them as wholly independent goddesses. Others feel that they are all various aspects of Frigg. Some of them are directly connected to Frigg, and at least one name is also used as a byname for Frigg. Mundal (1990) does mention that if these Asynjur are indeed hypostases of Frigg, "it is not likely that they belong to the last phase of paganism, but rather to an earlier period when Frigg was more central as a fertility goddess" (p. 305). Regardless of how one views them, they are each well worthy of discussion. Here, I will offer a brief description of these 12 Asynjur. I have chosen to list them in the order that they appear in *Gylfaginning* 35.

Sága

Sága follows right after Frigg as the second goddess mentioned in *Gylfaginning*. According to Sturluson, the name Sága means "see." If the name does mean "see" this could link Sága to a role as a seeress which would in turn connect her to Frigg. However, Simek (2007) notes that a link with "say, tell" is more probable. The meaning of "say, tell" could link the name Sága to the Icelandic prose works of the same name. As such, I picture Sága as a goddess who weaves legendary tales. Whether the name means "see" or "say" I still envision her has someone who possesses a vast knowledge that she willingly dispenses.

Sága is discussed in *Grímnismál* 7 of the *Poetic Edda* where it is said: "Sökkvabekk is the fourth, / where cool waves flow, / And amid their murmur it stands; / There daily do Othin / and Sága drink / In gladness from cups of gold" (Bellows, 1936, p. 89). In *Gylfaginning* the hall of Sága is mentioned by name again. Here it is simply stated to be a large dwelling. Simek (2007) translates Sokkvabekk to mean either "sunken bank" or "treasure bank" which would seem to relate her hall to one in marsh land or near some other body of water (p. 297). This is reminiscent of Frigg and her hall Fensalir. These instances, combined with Sága's connection to drinking with Odin, has led many to see Sága as a byname for Frigg (Näsström, 1995, p. 100 and Simek, 2007, p. 274).

Whether Sága is completely independent of Frigg, or a byname for her, she is well worthy of praise and worship in her own right. I picture Sága swapping epic stories with the great Odin in her hall. As the word *saga* can relate to stories of heroic legend, I see the goddess Sága as a record keeper of such events. History was the first subject to spark my scholarly interests in life. It is because of this that Sága has been placed in an ever-growing position of prominence in my life. Finally, as the designated family genealogist, it is her aid that I seek when engaging in such pursuits.

Eir

The Asynja who is listed third is Eir, and here it is stated that "she is the best physician" (Sturluson & Brodeur, 1916, p. 46). However, she also appears in some versions of the *Poetic Edda*. For instance, in *Svipdagsmol* 54, Eir is an assistant of Mengloth on the healing mountain of Lyfjaberg (Bellows, 1936). It is noteworthy that in this instance Eir has a connection to healing once again. Various commenters have compared Mengloth with either Freyja or Frigg. In Anthony Faulkes (1998) translation of the *Prose Edda*, Eir is also given as the name of a Valkyrie (*Skáldskaparmál* 75). Rudolf Simek (2007) notes this connection, and he goes on to speculate that this may be her original function. In the same chapter of the *Prose Edda*, Eir is noticeably absent among the goddesses that are named in the previous section. Aside from this, not much else is known of Eir, though many connect with her today as a healing goddess. In fact, according to Simek, her name is thought to be derived from the Old Norse *eir* meaning "help, mercy" further cementing her connection to this role (pp. 71-72).

Eir is a goddess whose presence is certainly felt in my life. As someone who suffers from numerous health issues, Eir has continued to provide me with guidance and support. While I am by no means a major health enthusiast, proper care for my body is a trend that amplifies with each passing year. I have chronic back pain which is a result of previous strains and multiple surgeries done to correct the situation. I often turn to Eir for both help and mercy when the pain reaches certain levels. It is also in times of medical issues for family members, including an emergency with one of my dogs, that I have prayed to Eir for safety and a speedy recovery process on their behalf. As I typically associate her with traditional healing methods, I feel that a knowledge of herb lore is beneficial in working with Eir.

Gefjun

Number four on the list is Gefjun. Simek (2007) translates the name Gefjun as "the giving one" (p. 102). In *Glyfaginning* 35 it is said that Gefjun "she is a virgin, and they that die maidens attend her" (Sturluson & Brodeur, 1916, p. 46). Unlike the previous goddesses listed, Gefjun appears in her own myth. In *Gylfaginning* 1 of the *Prose Edda* Sturluson tells the story of King Gylfi who made a deal with Gefjun. For the pleasure of her company, he would give her whatever size land she could plow in the timeframe of a day and a night. Gefjun happened to have four sons with a jotunn that are said to be oxen. They were able to dig so deep that they cut the land loose from Sweden and dragged it westward out into the sea forming the island of Zealand.

This same tale, or a version of it, is told in the *Ynglinga Saga* of the *Heimskringla*. In this version, Gefjun is sent by Odin to procure new lands. She sets out and arrives at King Gylfi's who gives her some land to plough. Then she ventures off to Jotunheim to mate with a jotunn and has four sons with him. Next, Gefjun transforms the sons into oxen, and then takes them to plough the land which is subsequently broken off transforming into the island. She eventually settles down and marries Skjold, a son of Odin. This version even comes with a song that Sturluson says Bragi the Old sings that goes as follows:

Gefion from Gylve drove away,
To add new land to Denmark's sway --
Blythe Gefion ploughing in the smoke
That steamed up from her oxen-yoke:
Four heads, eight forehead stars had they,
Bright gleaming, as she ploughed away;

Dragging new lands from the deep main
To join them to the sweet isle's plain
(Sturluson & Laing, 1844).

It is interesting to note here that Gefjun bearing children with a jotunn is quite outside the norm. While it is common for the gods to have sex with jotunn, the goddesses do not. In fact, oftentimes, such as the case of Freyja, the story involves keeping a specific jotunn from sleeping with the goddess in question. I feel this proves that Gefjun must be a particularly powerful Goddess who is able to choose who she wishes to have sex with even if it is a jotunn. In addition, according to this tale Gefjun has strong agricultural ties that make her a standout among members of Frigg's court. One could seek her intervention in the productivity of the land.

Gefjun also plays a part in *Lokasenna*. This is the poem in which Loki taunts the gods and goddesses with insults, many of which are quite personal. During Loki's tirade, Gefjun interjects trying to stop the dispute. Loki silences Gefjun and says that he knows Gefjun has slept with a young man for a piece of jewelry. Odin then says that Loki is mad for trying to anger Gefjun and states: "I think she foresees the fates / of all living things / as well as I do" (Crawford, 2015, p. 105). We see here that Gefjun has slept with someone for jewelry, and that she has the gift of prophecy. These are both similar to traits that Frigg possesses.

Gefjun also appears in later works. For instance, in *Vǫlsa þáttr*, a short story occurring in *Óláfs saga helga*, her name is invoked. It is a rather interesting invocation where the daughter of a thrall swears an oath to Gefjun on a horse penis. This oath goes as follows: "I swear by Gefjun and the other gods that I take the red phallus being forced to do so" (Näsström, 1995, p. 100). As described in Chapter 2, Gefjun is used to replace Athena in the *Trójumanna Saga*. Though she is later replaced herself with Frigg, it is still an interesting scenario. If she is indeed the intended representation of Athena, then Gefjun may have roles connected to both wisdom and battle. The interchanging of the names could indicate that at least this author viewed them as similar deities; unless this was done in error.

It was an even more common practice in translated Latin legends for Gefjun to be a translation for the goddess Diana (Mundal, 1990). This may mean that Gefjun has connections with hunting, wild places, and animals. At the very least, we can recognize that Gefjun has a link with oxen. We must also keep in mind here that another name for Freyja is the very similar Gefn. As Simek (2007) points out, this is thought to have a very similar meaning of "giver" in Old Norse (p. 102). If Gefjun and Gefn are the same this is yet another link between Frigg and Freyja.

I would say that out of all the Asynjur in Frigg's court it is Gefjun who acts the most independently. At the very least, she seems to feature the most prominently in the lore. The very fact that she features in her own myth at all is indicative of the power and prestige that she possesses both then and now. I feel that Gefjun straddles the line between Frigg and Freyja. She simultaneously shares qualities with both while also retaining her own sovereignty to a large degree.

Fulla

The fifth goddess listed is Fulla. She is attested to several times in the lore. Fulla is perhaps the goddess with the closest relationship to Frigg out of anyone in her court. As highlighted in Chapter 1, Fulla may in fact be a sister of Frigg. If the Volla spoken of in the *Second Merseburg Incantation* is indeed Fulla then we also see in her a role as a healer. Fulla is said to be a virgin goddess though what is implied by that is unknown. It most likely has a meaning of unmarried as opposed to sexually. We know, for instance, that Gefjun has a sexual relationship in *Gylfaginning* and yet she is still implied to be a virgin. Unique among the Asynjur we are given a very brief physical description of Fulla. In *Glyfaginning* it is said that Fulla wears her hair falling freely with a gold band around her head. We also learn that she is the keeper of Frigg's secrets, carrier of her ashen box, and looks after her footwear.

Simek (2007) notes that the name Fulla is used in kennings for both "gold" and "woman" in skaldic poetry (p. 96). She is also mentioned later in the *Prose Edda* as a goddess in *Skáldskaparmál* 1 and 75. In the first scenario she attends a feast where the god Aegir is the guest of honor. Fulla and Gefjun are the only handmaidens on this list. They are accompanied by Frigg, Freyja, Idunn, Gerd, Sigyn, and Nanna. This would seem to place Fulla in fairly high regard. As discussed in Chapter 2, Fulla is highlighted in the introduction to *Grímnismál* of the *Poetic Edda* where she directly assists Frigg in her deception of Odin.

I do indeed feel that Fulla and Frigg have a close relationship, probably closer than any of the other Asynjur. She appears as Frigg's closest friend. She is someone Frigg trusts with the most crucial of duties. The betrayal of Odin in *Grímnismál* is an attestation to the lengths that she will go to for Frigg. The fact that Frigg sends her on such a risky venture also displays the level of trust Frigg has in Fulla's abilities. As a keeper of objects and secrets, Fulla displays the characteristics of a divine confidante. I sense in her a guardian of special objects, particularly of a spiritual nature.

I have a box of various spiritual items such as several types of jewelry. It is in Fulla that I entrust its safekeeping. As the name Fulla implies abundance, I see this as representative of the gifts she bestows on us. I have also read of many that see in Fulla the path of connections between two or more women. While I cannot speak from experience, I can see this to be a fitting role. Personally, I have found that all my best friends have been women for much of my life. I can see Fulla even playing at least a small part in these friendships that I hold so dear as well.

Sjöfn

The seventh Asynja listed, after Freyja in the sixth spot, is Sjöfn. Sturluson states that Sjöfn is tasked with turning thoughts of both men and women toward love. He goes on to state; "from her name love-longing is called *sjafni*" (Sturluson & Brodeur, 1916, p. 46). Sjöfn is also listed among the Asynjur of *Skáldskaparmál* 75. Sjöfn is scarcely attested to outside of this, though Simek (2007) notes that she is mentioned a few times in skaldic poetry. Simek also states the name itself may be derived from either *sefi* "sense" or *sefi* "relation" and as such connects her to relationships (p. 286).

I envision Sjöfn as overseeing the constant state of love in all relationships. Whether it is the love between family members, the love existing between friends, or the love between two soul mates, Sjöfn oversees the love between these individuals. It is even during matters of dispute with someone I care for that I pray to Sjöfn. I do this in the hope of turning these occasionally harmful emotions to ones of love and reconciliation. She is the embodiment of love that seeks to sustain relationships in their many forms.

Lofn

The eighth spot belongs to Lofn, and she is another goddess that is directly connected to Frigg. Sturluson says that she is gentle and good, and that she has the permission of both Odin and Frigg to arrange relationships; even if those relationships have been banned for one reason or another. This can include a wide array of relationships depending on various elements such as religious background, race, social status, and innumerable other differences. In the *Prose Edda* the name Lofn is said to mean 'loving' and that the word *lof* means both "permission" and "high praise" (Sturluson & Byock, 2005, pg. 43). Simek (2007) translates the name from Old Norse as "the comforter, the mild" (p. 190).

Lofn is the goddess of one's true love, independent of persecution and judgement. Unbeknownst to me, I have sought out a connection with Lofn early into my youth. As a person who identifies as queer, I now feel a special relationship with Lofn. As my marriage was seen, and still is seen by many, as something to be banned this is an obvious connection to make. While I did not have the wherewithal to invoke Lofn at my wedding, I have since then sought her guidance and her support. In recent years we have seen the resurgence of a hate fueled political climate that has sought to admonish anything viewed as "other" in our societies. This goes without saying that, where I am from in the United States, we are more fortunate than many other locations around the world. If you find yourself in a relationship that is not seen as permissible, it is to Lofn that you should guide your prayers.

Vár

The ninth Asynja given is Vár. According to the *Prose Edda* (Sturluson & Byock, 2005) and Simek (2007) the name Vár is believed to mean "beloved." She seems to oversee oaths and contracts made between individuals. She is also known to take vengeance out on those who break these agreements. Besides being listed among the goddesses in *Gylfaginning* 35 she is also listed among the goddesses in *Skáldskaparmál* 75. Lastly, her name is invoked in *Poetic Edda* poem *Þrymskviða*. This is the famous story involving Thor where he attempts to recover his hammer, Mjolnir, from the jotunn Þrym by dressing as Freyja to wed the jotunn. During the ceremony Þrym states: "May Vár, goddess of / wedding vows, bless us" (Crawford, 2015, p. 121).

Vár, as a goddess of oaths and love, is an obvious connection to wedding vows; as given in the previous example. My marriage plays an integral part of my life. I am someone who had to wait before changes were made so that I was legally permitted to marry. It is perhaps because of this that I take my wedding vows so seriously. They really mean something to me so it should come as no surprise that Vár serves such an important part in my life. Vows, and any oath really, should hold a significant amount of weight for us as individuals. Our word is worth nothing if we are unable to hold on to the oaths that we speak. Vár oversees those oaths and assures that we keep them.

Vör

The tenth goddess on the list is Vör, meaning "the careful one" (Simek, 2007, p. 368). Sturluson writes about Vör stating she; "is so knowledgeable and inquires so deeply that nothing can be hidden from her. Hence the expression that a woman becomes 'aware' [vor] of what she learns" (Sturluson & Byock, 2005, p. 43). She is again listed by Sturluson in *Skáldskaparmál* 75 in the list of goddesses found there. Aside from these two mentions she is given in kennings for "woman" and nothing more in the written record.

Vör is a goddess of wisdom, but of wisdom that is hidden. She is not what is written, but what is seen with the mind's eye. Vör is intuition, perhaps even specializing in 'women's intuition' as it were. That said, I feel that Vör can oversee matters relating to divination for any of us regardless of the confines of gender identity. Like Frigg, Vör is a seeress, but she is permitted to divulge what she knows. Seek out Vör's guidance when you seek to be aware, but just be careful of what it is you wish to hear.

Syn

The eleventh on this list is Syn. Sturluson writes of Syn in *Gylfaginning* 35 that; "She guards the doors in the hall and

71

locks out those who ought not enter. She is also appointed to defend cases that she wants to see refuted in the courts" (Sturluson & Byock, 2005, p. 43). Simek (2007) connects her name to both "refusal" and "denial" (p. 309). Simek also relates Syn to protective goddesses who are like the disir and Germanic matronae. She is also listed among the goddesses of *Skáldskaparmál* 75.

Syn is the guardian incarnate. When I am away from home, which as an agoraphobic is very rare, I ask for Syn to guard my home and my fur-children that may be left behind. Leaving my home behind is an enormous fear that I must contend with even if I am just planning to be away for a matter of moments; so, I cannot overstate the importance Syn has in my life. On a spiritual level, I personally invoke Syn in every ritual I perform to Frigg. I utilize her ability as a guardian to ward my sacred space prior to the ritual. Syn is also the guardian to personal boundaries that we may place on ourselves and onto others.

Hlín

Hlín is the twelfth Asynja that is given. Hlín is a goddess that can be directly connected to Frigg. In *Gylfaginning* 35 it is said that Frigg appoints Hlín to protect those Frigg chooses from danger. Byock relates that her name means "protector" and that the word *hleinir*, meaning "peace and quiet," derives from it (Sturluson & Byock, 2005, p. 43). Hlín appears in kennings in skaldic material 25 times (Näsström, 1995). Frigg herself is mentioned in kennings on only three occasions (Mundal, 1990). If Hlín is another name for Frigg, then both Frigg and Freyja are quite frequently used in this context. Simek (2007) seems confident in saying that Hlín is just another name for Frigg due to Hlín's occurrence in Völuspá where it serves as a byname for Frigg. He seems to feel that Sturluson misunderstood this reference and made the claim that she was an independent goddess (p. 153). Näsström also holds the opinion that Hlín is another name for Frigg (p. 100).

I can only speak from my experience and opinion when I say that I do feel that Hlín *can* be a byname for Frigg, but that is not *always* the case. I feel in the instance of Völuspá the intention was that Hlín failed in this instance to protect what Frigg had hoped she would. Thus, these were sorrows of both Frigg as well as Hlín. There may be a fine line between the pursuits of Syn and Hlín, but there is a difference. While Syn may guard the doors to keep us safe, it is Hlín that is standing by with weapon and shield in hand ready to fight. Petition Hlín when you need that extra push to stand up for what is right and just to protect those that you care about.

Snotra

Snotra is the thirteenth on the list in *Gylfaginning* 35. Snotra is also referenced in *Skáldskaparmál* 75 in the list of Asynjur. She is said by Sturluson to be both wise and courtly. He also adds that; "From her name comes the custom of calling a clever woman or man *snotr*" (Sturluson & Byock, 2005, p. 43). Simek (2007) seems to feel that Sturluson completely fabricated Snotra as she is not attested elsewhere. However, elsewhere in the same book, she is grouped by Simek with Sága, Hlín, Sjöfn, Vár, and Vör as "female protective goddesses...responsible for specific areas of the private sphere, and yet clear differences were made between them so that they are in many ways similar to the matrons" (p. 274).

I feel that the purview of Snotra involves both wisdom and knowledge. This is wisdom that we have accumulated, perhaps even in past lives, as well as the knowledge to understand just how to use such wisdom. Under this would certainly fall proper custom and manners of a courtly nature. As a student of life, Snotra plays an ever-important part in my daily activities.

I pray to her when I need that guidance to know the proper course of action in any given situation. I often refer to Snotra as the gracious one. Seek her out when you need a helping hand in this area of life. I feel that this is a quality severely lacking in our current world and her presence is much needed.

Gná

Finally, the fourteenth Asynja that is listed is Gná. As for this final goddess, Sturluson has much to say. Gná runs errands throughout the world for Frigg on a horse named Hofvarpnir, meaning "hoof-kicker (Sturluson & Byock, 2005, p. 43). Hofvarpnir can ride through the air and the sea. Sturluson states that at some point on her travels, she came across some Vanir who stated:

> "What flies there? / What fares there / or moving through the air?"
> She replied:
> "I fly not / though I fare / and move through the air / on Hofvarpnir, / the one whom Hamskerpir got / with Gardrofa" (p. 44)

Sturluson comments that "the custom of something gnaefir [looms] when it rises high" (p. 44). However, Simek (2007) feels that this connection is not correct but believes the names meaning is otherwise unknown. Simek does go on to mention the possibility of Gná as a "goddess of fullness" (p. 113).

Whether the name Gná implies fullness or not, I feel that her role is well understood. Gná is the messenger of Frigg willing to go to any lengths to relay her communications. In fact, communication is a great term to connect to Gná. In our high-speed world with an ability to communicate in the blink of an eye it is easy to take this for granted. However, it is more proper to keep in mind just how lucky we are. Even if communicating via text can leave something to be desired, we are truly fortunate to live in such an age. I see Gná as overseeing this function with the bonus of guiding our communications. That is to say Gná guides us with correct and right speech. In writing a book it was her that I often looked to so that she may guide my words to properly convey my message. I hope that she has proven to you a most useful guide in this regard.

Personal Take

Each of the preceding Asynjur have played at least some part in my practice. Some are more present than others in my daily spiritual work, but they are active in it nonetheless. As you can see, the specific identity of these Asynjur as fully independent deities is a bit murky. As a polytheist, I usually try and see each one as a unique goddess and honor them when appropriate. However, in practice it is a bit more nuanced than that. For instance, a few of them may simply be 'aspects' of Frigg, but I feel that still makes them worthy of veneration in their own right.

My own opinion of deities is very hard to describe, but even more so in the case of Frigg's royal court. I see each one as a unique entity able to manifest on their own. However, I do feel that some gods spring from other gods. While I may consider Frigg and Hlín to be individuals that can both exist at the same time and space; I also feel that Hlín is just one of the many manifestations of Frigg. The same could be said for each of these goddesses. In the case of Gefjun, I feel that she is an emanation of both Frigg and Freyja who can manifest freely and in the presence of both goddesses. I can pray to all three of these goddesses and, in a perfect world, could receive blessings from each of them separately.

I feel that, in the end, if we spend too much time trying to sort things out, we can drive ourselves mad. I do not think we are necessarily meant to be able to perfectly grasp the concept of deity. They are divine after all. It can be hard enough trying to figure out everyday people. The line between deities, spirits, jotunn, and various other entities is quite often blurry, and I am okay with that. I am just meant to put my trust in them, and honor them appropriately. I will leave it to those better versed than myself to try and define them.

Chapter 6

Acts of Devotion to Frigg

I have chosen to dedicate the last chapter of this book to the practical applications that you can employ on your spiritual journey with Frigg. I plan to cover a few topics here to get you started. I will begin with altar construction and what that can entail. Next, I will discuss the topic of offerings. Then I will go over prayers and offer up some of my own prayers that I have written in dedication to Frigg. Finally, I will end with a selection of sacred days that hold some importance in my personal relationship with Frigg.

Altars

Altars are important because they offer us a focal point when doing prayer and ritual in the home. It is easy to get distracted, and I personally want all my attention to be on the deity I am offering to in each situation. These suggestions will be specifically aimed for an altar to Frigg, though you could easily exchange items more suitable for another god or goddess. The construction of an altar can take many forms. There really is no one right way to do this so let your mind run free. That said, I usually have a couple of suggestions when asked.

The first thing you will need is a solid, durable, and flat surface. This can be a dining room table, an end table, nightstand, or something as simple as a wooden crate. Aside from that, the only limit here is your imagination. As I said, I would recommend something that is solidly constructed. You may have a burning candle on it, so you do not want it to tip over and catch fire. If you choose, either out of necessity or aesthetics, you can include an altar cloth over the top of it. This is not a requirement, however. I have several altars throughout my home, and I have utilized old, repurposed end tables for several of them and a few wall-mounted shelves as well. I include an altar cloth on a couple of them.

The next thing I would suggest is an image of Frigg. This can be a symbolic object that reminds you of Frigg such as a set of keys, or something more literal. Again, this helps to focus. There are many beautiful artistic depictions of Frigg online. Find your favorite one and purchase it if you can. I feel it is important to support independent artists. However, some images are in the public domain, so they are free to use. Additionally, if your budget permits, there exists an array of gorgeous statues on the market today in various sizes. I have a slight addiction to deity statues that drives my husband batty. I currently possess six of Frigg alone-more than any other deity. In my defense, one was sent to me by mistake and the designer told me to keep it before sending me the correct one.

The third recommendation I will make is an offering dish. This can be a plate, bowl, cup, or whatever else will suit your needs. Just be mindful of how you will use it. The last thing you will want to do is find a beautiful offering plate that you designate for Frigg, only to find yourself constantly wanting to make liquid offerings. I include a bowl on several of my altars. This covers most of my bases. Whether I choose liquid or solid offerings the bowls always serve the correct purpose. You also are not required to run out and purchase brand new offering dishes. You can always find special pieces second hand. In addition, I find that slowly acquiring any of these altar items gives them a much more personal touch.

Fourth and fifth is something appropriate for burning. One for a candle and one for incense. I highly suggest purchasing items that are specifically designed for their purpose. Anything that burns can obviously start a fire. Making wise purchases that can withstand the heat of candles and incense is of the utmost importance. The candle is used to ward the sacred space and offer another focus aid. The incense I utilize for both a method to carry my prayers to Frigg, and as an offering. These things being said, if you find yourself in a situation where you are not permitted to burn things then by all means abstain from doing so. Whether it is a landlord and tenant situation, or you can not burn things for health reasons then those factors come first. Whatever your reasons they are important. You will not anger Frigg for not partaking in burning some incense and a candle. Remember there are alternatives. For instance, it is quite common to see battery powered candles these days. These are excellent substitutes that should serve your purposes just fine. As for the incense, you can choose an array of other offerings in its place, and its workings to guide my prayers is more symbolic than anything.

Personally, these are all the items that I find as required for my spiritual work. As I said at the beginning of this section, the only limit is your imagination. This is your personal working space with Frigg. Craft it in whatever way you see fit. These items simply serve as a minimum for my practices, but you may belong to other spiritual paths that require, or suggest, completely different items, and that is just fine.

Offerings

Offerings are an important part of working with Frigg, or any deity for that matter. It is all part of the gifting cycle. If you are dedicated to her and want to show her true praise, then making an offering is the easiest step that you can take. It shows her that you appreciate the part she plays in your life, and if you ever need something in return, she is more likely to return a gift to you if you participate in this cycle. The subject of offerings can include any number of items. I have yet to find an offering that has been rejected. Though I am sure there are probably some offerings that are less suited than others. Here I will offer up some of the basics that I have utilized in the past.

The first item that I use for offerings is incense. This is a simple gift that Frigg seems to enjoy. If I am simply giving a prayer of praise or of thanksgiving, then incense makes a very quick and easy offering. As I previously stated, incense may not be for you. I myself love incense, but I am also prone to getting headaches if the scent is not right. I do recommend higher end incense as I feel that it is both a better offering and less likely to give me a headache. I typically use pure incense made from natural ingredients that is coreless. I find that when the incense is burnt on a stick, I am more likely to be sensitive to it. A simple search for coreless incense will yield some great results. As far as the scent itself I find that what is preferential to you is suitable for Frigg. I do not think that Frigg has any desire for us to suffer through undesirable scents that make us uncomfortable.

Next up is beverage and food offerings. Appropriate liquids that can be offered include alcohol-based drinks such as wine, mead, and beer. I would opt for a good quality, but nothing that is going to cause you financial strain. I personally do not drink so it is rare that I offer alcohol. However, it is important to note that in the past the brewing of alcohol was typically the work of the women of the household. So, I think this makes an excellent offering for Frigg. Alcohol free apple cider is a great substitute. Additionally, as a goddess of domestic work, milk makes a great offering. Food is a broad subject, but I will say that homemade baked goods are most suitable for Frigg. Fresh baked bread is an offering I have made on an occasion or two. Herbs and spices can be given as well. Cinnamon, cardamom, and allspice will work great.

Another option is to dedicate you work in service to Frigg. When I am doing my chores around the house, I do it for my own well-being, but the work is dedicated to Frigg. Offering your service of a clean and healthy home is a pure act of devotion to do it in her name. This is especially true when I am doing crafting jobs such as soap making and weaving. These both hold a special connection for me where Frigg is concerned. Finally, you can donate your time to various causes that are important to you. Volunteering your time working with children and animals is very appropriate and in line with things that Frigg would hold dear.

As you can see, there are many options to offer up to Frigg. These are simply the most common ways that I enter into a gifting cycle with her. So far, I have yet to offer anything that was outright rejected on her behalf. If you find value in an object, then chances are good that Frigg will find the value in it as well.

Prayers

Prayers form an important aspect of honoring the gods. Yes, Norse pagans of the past did pray. I will offer a few basic prayers as an example, but first I thought I would offer a basic prayer format so that you can write your own. The procedure that I utilize is fairly simple in structure and goes as follows:

1. Invocation: This is the step where you formally address Frigg by calling her name. I usually follow this with a few proper kennings for her as well that are aimed at the particular area of focus for the prayer.
2. Petition: This is the portion of the prayer where you mention why you are praying to Frigg. This could be a prayer of praise, or a request. In this step you make your intentions known.
3. Offering: This step is optional. I do suggest that if you are making a request for something, and you are able to, that you make an offering. If it is a prayer of praise, it may not be necessary. Though, if you are offering praise because you have received something, and you feel it may be Frigg's doing, then an offering may be appropriate.

4. Closing: This is where you say something simple to signify that the prayer has come to its conclusion.

You can choose to write your prayers out ahead of time or recite them in the moment. If you are just starting out, then you may choose to write them out beforehand. However, if you are comfortable, feel free to just speak what is in your heart. I have certain prayers that I perform regularly and those were initially written out, but now that I have the relationship with Frigg that I do I am comfortable just speaking with her off the cuff.

What follows are just a few examples of prayers to Frigg. I will begin by offering a simple prayer of praise. This is a general, all-purpose prayer to thank Frigg for gifts that you may have received on her behalf. The second prayer will be one for good health. This could be for continued health of the needed blessing of health. The third prayer is a general prayer for help or guidance over a matter that is important to you.

Prayer of Praise
I pray to you, Frigg, mother of bright Baldr.
Queen of the Æsir and of the Asynjur,
All-Mother and Hearth-Mother.
In your divine blessings, you have guided me,
with your hand, you have gifted me.
It is with my words that I thank you for prosperity,
of mind, body and soul that you lift.
May continued gifts be exchanged,
and may you take them with open arms.
In your name I pray.
Hail to you, Frigg!

Prayer for Good Health
I come before you, Frigg,
who with Fulla sang a healing spell,

82

for Baldr's horse.
Divine Healer,
the one who has helped her children,
so many times, before.
That you deem me worthy,
I ask for blessing of good health.
I make you this offering today.
(Make Offering)
May you accept it with my good intentions,
And may it serve you well.
A gift for a gift,
To you I pray.

Prayer for Guidance/Help
Frigg, of the halls of Fensalir.
You are the weaver of peace,
she who knows all the fates.
Great beloved, wisest Asynja,
I ask that guidance you impart.
This is my hour of great need,
and in you I put my hearts trust.
I make this offering to you,
so that tomorrow, I may offer more.
(Make Offering)
I hope that this offer is worthy,
and that it is well received.
I speak these words,
and in your name, I pray.

As you can see, the prayer does not need to be perfectly written in the manner I outlined. However, they each contain the elements that I listed in my formula for prayers. I feel that these are general prayers that can work in several situations. You can easily alter a word or two to suit your needs. Hopefully, you will be able to compose your own prayers in no time.

Holy Days

I feel that sacred days can be a highly personal matter. It is great if we have historical precedence for a specific holy day, but this is not always a possibility. Considering such evidence, I am all for finding days that mean something special to you and celebrating Frigg then. To my understanding, there has been no feast day found that was dedicated specifically to the honor of Frigg. That is not to say one did not exist in the past, it just means that we have no modern record of it. Taking all that into account, there are a few special days on the calendar that I think would have been important to Frigg. With that said, I do recommend celebrating Frigg everyday as I feel she can greatly enrich your life.

You may notice that a couple of these following holy days fall on or near holidays from different religious traditions. I do not do this to hijack these other faiths, or to simple merge them with little regard for the source tradition. I grew up in a very secular household. We placed little religious emphasis on any holiday. As my polytheist practice grew, some of these dates felt like a natural time to celebrate. They have just become a part of my practice. I choose to make them part of a modern celebration in honor of Frigg. It is my hope that you find ways to celebrate her that feel like natural extensions to your spiritual path.

Mothers-Night

The first day that I connect to Frigg, and perhaps the most important for me, is the Anglo-Saxon Mōdraniht, or "Mothers-Night." You will most likely find a few different dates to honor this holy festival. When you decide to celebrate it is entirely up to you. The Christian monk Bede recorded that it was held the same night as Christmas Eve (Pollington, 2011, p. 328). However,

I have heard of people choosing to celebrate on the eve of the winter solstice, or the night of the winter solstice as well. This festival is most likely connected to the Matron cults of the West Germanic peoples (Simek, 2007). Bearing this in mind, I feel that this is the perfect night to honor Frigg as both the All-Mother and Hearth-Mother. The first time I ever read about Mothers-Night I remember thinking to myself that it seemed tailor-made for Frigg. I have honored her on that night ever since.

The festival is closely linked in time, and probably by its festivities, with the sacred holiday of Yule. I do typically celebrate this festival so that it coincides with Christmas Eve. Christmas Day is still spent at my parents' house with my siblings and our respective spouses. That makes Christmas Eve more special for my husband and I, as well as for Frigg. Since we are busy the following day, this is the night that I exchange gifts with my husband. Aside from that, I spend the day in reverence of Frigg and my ancestral mothers. I typically make a very small feast for my husband and me. Then I will take a portion and make an offering to Frigg. I try and spend the day in prayer and self-reflection.

Hearth and Home Festival/Candlemas/ (Disting-See Below)

I realize I do not have a proper title for this day, but regardless it is a very special one for me. I tend to celebrate this day near the beginning of February. This is very much a festival of my home and Frigg as its designated guardian. This is when I kick off my annual spring cleaning. This may seem like a strange way to celebrate, but it feels good to physically and spiritually cleanse my home at this time. This may last several weeks depending on what else is going on in my life at that time. This day is not only about hard work, however. As with other holy days I make offerings to Frigg at this time. I will usually perform a cleansing ritual to kick things off, and once I have completed my tasks, I will do one more.

Midsummer/Litha

To me, Midsummer has always been a great time to celebrate the Earth's fertility. This is when many plants are at their peak in the growing season. As such, it is the perfect time to celebrate Frigg in her role as a goddess of fertility. While the heat may be extreme for many of us during this day, it is a great time to get out and tend to our gardens. I feel that Frigg has a vested interest in seeing them prosper. I have had some vegetable and leafy greens ready at this time of year in the past and they make for a wonderful salad in honor of Frigg. Just make sure and leave a bit for an offering for her while you are at it.

Hlafmas/Lammas

This day is a harvest festival. In many Pagan circles it is the first of three such holy days. Traditionally, held in the beginning of August, this day is particularly connected to the grain harvest. This makes it quite a suitable holy day for baking! As a goddess of both the home and fertility this feast pulls double duty. If anything in my garden needs tending, I will tend to it, but this day-like the calendrical opposite day of Candlemas-is one suitable for home and hearth duties. Prayers are given and a ritual is performed, but an important gift of fresh baked bread is also offered to Frigg on this day.

Dísablót

Another similarly themed holy day as Mothers-Night is known as Dísablót, meaning 'sacrifice to the disir'. The disir are usually held to be female deities or powerful spirits. There are a couple of different dates for this sacred day as well. The *Víga-Glúms Saga* gives a start date at the beginning of winter, which in this instance correlates to mid-October (Simek, 2007, p. 60). *Egil's*

Saga references a similarly timed autumn celebration. Again, it is entirely up to you when you celebrate. Some wish to keep it as historically accurate as possible, but this is not required. To be honest, I typically try and hold Dísablót on either the first full moon after the autumnal equinox or on the Celtic Samhain. Growing up, this was always my favorite time of year. When I first approached Celtic Polytheism this all came full circle for me. This way I get to continue that tradition. I see this night as the perfect time to celebrate not only Frigg, but her entire court. They are all powerful goddesses that deserve their day of celebration. I will light candles and say prayers to each of them in their honor. In addition, I once again honor my female ancestors on this day.

As a side note, there is also the similarly named Disting that is held in Uppsala Sweden annually. It essentially means the "Thing of the Dis." In the *Saga of Olaf Haraldson*, Sturluson writes that it took place in 'Goa Month' which roughly corresponds to the modern time period of late February and early March. Sturluson adds that: "After Christianity had taken root in Svithjod, and the kings would no longer dwell in Upsala, the market-time was moved to Candlemas, and it has since continued so, and it lasts only three days" (Sturluson & Laing, 1844). This provides an alternate time to hold this celebration; which coincidentally falls near the hearth and home festival that I already celebrate.

Personal Take

This whole chapter has really been a 'personal take' in a manner of speaking, so I do not have much to add here. It is my hope that you took away many lessons and ideas for how you can personally honor Frigg. The section on altars comes from my personal experience of tending to polytheist centered sacred spaces, and it has served me well for two decades. If nothing else, I can say I am versed in altar construction. Just remember, take your time to really create a space that you love, and Frigg will appreciate. This will be your spiritual oasis.

The offerings and prayer section are both based as closely on historical precedence that I could come across. They have also played a part in my spiritual life for many, many years. Please do not limit yourself to strictly what I listed. If you wish, start with something I mentioned for your first offering as you have someone that can vouch for their effectiveness. However, while they do make great first offerings, there really is not much that Frigg would reject in my experience. Be creative and be heartfelt and you will not go wrong.

Finally, the section on holy days is based in part on the historical record, but perhaps more importantly, it is also based on personal practice. These are days that I have come to hold in high regard, and I feel that they have been greeted with a warm welcome by Frigg. There are, of course, other holy days that you can choose to honor Frigg as well. Find the times that mean something to you and your relationship with Frigg. That will make them all the more special. May these examples lead you well on your journey.

Conclusion

Frigg comes to us today as one of the most important deities of Germanic Polytheism. Whatever you label your particular tradition, if it is in any way connected to the pantheon of the Germanic people, then Frigg can bring much to your life. Far too often, she is overlooked. Perhaps, as a guardian of marriage and the home, she is not as flashy as other members of the Æsir. We must remember that she is those things, which are of great importance, and she is so much more.

As the leader of a bevy of Asynjur, Frigg holds numerous qualifications to enrich our lives. She is the tireless defender of children, and she is a weaver of peace. She is a dedicated goddess of marriage, and she still knows how to fulfill her sexual desires. She is the goddess who knows the fates of all, but she never reveals what it is that she knows. She is a goddess of seemingly paradoxical traits, and she maintains devout in her convictions.

Frigg is a guiding light in the lives of many, and for good reason. The traits alluded to in the last paragraph illustrate why. Through all her amazing characteristics, she is reachable to us all. I can never see her turning away from anyone, save for those of the most ill intentions. The close allies that she has in her royal court show her most capable of great bonds of friendship. Her compassionate championing of Baldr, and her steadfast love of her husband also lend to this idea.

So, what if you are unmarried and find little desire to keep up with your housework routinely? I am still sure that Frigg can prove a positive force in your life. I have heard on any number of occasions that Frigg is a goddess for women. While I would agree with this, I also feel that she has provided me numerous gifts without me fulfilling that role. I have seen her called a goddess of children and childbirth. Again, I would agree with this, but counter that is not a role I have any personal connection to. I found other ways to connect with these same roles in a manner that is unique to my perspective.

From the earliest sources to the Edda's and sagas we have witnessed a goddess of tremendous power and varied functions. She is a goddess who is molded by her relationships, but not entirely defined by them. Frigg is the daughter of Fjörgynn, the wife of Odin, the mother of Baldr, the mother-in-law of Nanna, the stepmother to Thor and numerous other gods. Frigg is the divine leader of Sága, Eir, Gefjun, Fulla, Sjöfn, Lofn, Vár, Vör, Syn, Hlín, Snotra, and Gná. Maybe they are divine hypostases of her, or maybe they simply have a relationship that is destined to lay beyond our comprehension for all time.

Let Frigg into your life and see the gifts that our beloved Asynja can bestow. Pray to her. Make offerings to her. Meditate on her. Whatever you do, do not make this your last stop. I sincerely hope that this was either the beginning of your relationship with Frigg, or just a stop along the way. It is not meant to be a final destination. This book contains information I have collected along the way on my journey. A journey that still goes on today and will continue past the writing of this book. It is my experience of Frigg, but chances are yours will differ in a great many ways. This is to be expected of a goddess of such vast skills and qualities that they could not be contained within these pages. Hail Frigg: Beloved Queen of Asgard!

About the Author

Ryan McClain is a multi-traditional polytheist and animist; though his path is predominantly influenced by both Gaulish and Germanic hearth cultures. Several deities are a consistent part of his practice, but of particular importance are the goddesses Abnoba and Frigg, having honored them for three and seven years respectively. Ryan earned his degree in 2010 in General Studies for the express purpose of gaining a broad base of knowledge. Since that time, he has dedicated himself to many pursuits of study via books, the internet, experimentation, meditation, prayer, and any other means possible. Ryan resides in a small town in Indiana where he lives with his husband and their loveable dogs, fiercely independent rabbit, and wacky bearded dragon.

References

Ásdísardóttir, I. (2006). Frigg and Freyja: One Great Goddess or Two? In *The Fantastic in Old Norse/Icelandic Literature; Sagas and the British Isles: Preprint Papers of the 13th International Saga Conference Durham and York, 6th–12th August 2006* (pp. 417-424).

Bellows, H. A. (1936). *The Poetic Edda*. The American-Scandinavian Foundation.

Byock, J. L. (1990). *The Saga of the Volsungs: The Norse Epic of Sigurd the Dragon Slayer*. University of California Press.

Crawford, J. (2015). *The Poetic Edda: Stories of the Norse Gods and Heroes*. Hackett Publishing Company, Inc.

Davidson, H. E. (1993). *The Lost Beliefs of Northern Europe*. Routledge.

Davidson, H. E. (2001). *Roles of the Northern Goddess*. Routledge.

Elton, O. (Trans.). (1905). *The Nine Books of the Danish History of Saxo Grammaticus*. Norrœna Society.

Grimm, J. (1882). *Teutonic mythology*. (J. S. Stallybrass, Trans.). G. Bell.

Grundy, S. (2002). Freyja and Frigg. In S. Billington &; M. Green (Eds.), *The Concept of the Goddess* (pp. 56–66). essay, Taylor and Francis.

Herbert, K. (2010). *Looking for the Lost Gods of England*. Anglo-Saxon Books.

Hyltén-Cavallius, G. O. (1922). *Wärend och wirdarne* (Vol. 2). PA Norstedt.

Ingham, M. F. (1985). *The goddess Freyja and other female figures in Germanic mythology and folklore* (thesis). Cornell University.

Kershaw, N. (1921). *Stories and Ballads of the Far Past: Translated from the Norse (Icelandic and Faroese) with introductions and notes*. Cambridge University Press.

McKinnell, J., Ashurst, D., Kick, D., &; Asdisardottir, I. (2006). Frigg and Freyja: One Great Goddess or Two? In *The fantastic in Old Norse/Icelandic literature*. Preprint papers of the 13th International Saga Conference Durham and York, 6th-12th August, 2006 (pp. 417–423). essay, The Centre for Medieval and Renaissance Studies.

Mundal, E. (1990). *The Position of the Individual Gods and Goddesses in Various Types of Sources - with Special Reference to the Female Divinities*. Scripta Instituti Donneriani Aboensis, 13, 294–315. https://doi.org/10.30674/scripta.67181

Näsström Britt-Mari. (1995). *Freyja: The Great Goddess of the North*. Department of History of Religions, University of Lund.

Paulus. (1907). *History of the Langobards*. (W. D. Foulke, Trans.). The Department of History, University of Pennsylvania. Retrieved June 16, 2022, from https://archive.org/details/historyoflangoba00pauluoft/page/n3/mode/2up.

Pollington, S. (2011). *The Elder Gods: The Otherworld of Early England*. Anglo-Saxon Books.

Ross, M. C., Quinn, J., Heslop, K., Wills, T., &; Brink, S. (2007). How Uniform was the Old Norse Religion? *In Learning and understanding in the Old Norse World: Essays in Honour of Margaret Clunies Ross* (pp. 105–136). essay, Brepols.

Sigurðsson, J. (1848). *Trojumanna Saga*. The Royal Nordic Antiquarian Society.

Simek, R. (2007). *Dictionary of northern mythology*. (A. Hall, Trans.). D.S. Brewer. (Original work published 1984)

Smiley, J., Kellogg, R., &; Scudder, B. (2000). Egil's Saga. In *Sagas of Icelanders*. essay, Viking Penguin.

Sturluson, S. (1844). *The Heimskringla*. (S. Laing, Trans.). Musaicum Books.

Sturluson, S. (1916). *The Prose Edda*. (A. G. Brodeur, Trans.). The American-Scandinavian Foundation.

Sturluson, S. (1998). *Edda*. (A. Faulkes, Trans.). J.M. Dent.

Sturluson, S. (2005). *The Prose Edda: Norse mythology*. (J. L. Byock, Trans.). Penguin Books.

Turville-Petre, G. E. O. (1964). *Myth and Religion of the North: The Religion of Ancient Scandinavia*. Greenwood Press Publishers.

You may also like

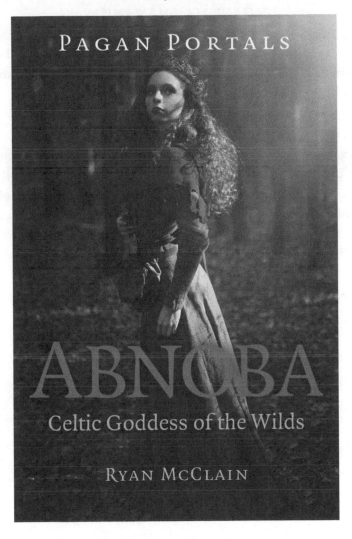

Abnoba - Celtic Goddess of the Wilds
Take an investigative journey to connect with Abnoba,
the mysterious woodland goddess of the ancient Gauls

978-1-80341-024-1 (Paperback)
978-1-80341-025-8 (e-book)

The Morrigan
Meeting the Great Queens
Morgan Daimler
*Ancient and enigmatic, the Morrigan reaches out to us.
On shadowed wings and in raven's call, meet the ancient Irish
goddess of war, battle, prophecy, death, sovereignty, and magic.*
Paperback: 978-1-78279-833-0 ebook: 978-1-78279-834-7

The Awen Alone
Walking the Path of the Solitary Druid
Joanna van der Hoeven
*An introductory guide for the solitary Druid, The Awen Alone
will accompany you as you explore, and seek out your own
place within the natural world.*
Paperback: 978-1-78279-547-6 ebook: 978-1-78279-546-9

Moon Magic
Rachel Patterson
*An introduction to working with the phases of the Moon,
what they are and how to live in harmony with the lunar
year and to utilise all the magical powers it provides.*
Paperback: 978-1-78279-281-9 ebook: 978-1-78279-282-6

Hekate
A Devotional
Vivienne Moss
*Hekate, Queen of Witches and the Shadow-Lands, haunts the pages
of this devotional bringing magic and enchantment into your lives.*
Paperback: 978-1-78535-161-7 ebook: 978-1-78535-162-4

Readers of ebooks can buy or view any of these bestsellers by clicking on the live link in the title. Most titles are published in paperback and as an ebook. Paperbacks are available in traditional bookshops. Both print and ebook formats are available online.

Find more titles and sign up to our readers' newsletter http://www.johnhuntpublishing.com/paganism

For video content, author interviews and more, please subscribe to our YouTube channel.

MoonBooksPublishing

Follow us on social media for book news, promotions and more:

Facebook: Moon Books Publishing

Instagram: @moonbooksjhp

Twitter: @MoonBooksJHP

Tik Tok: @moonbooksjhp